EXAM REVISION

A2 Law
Tort Law

Emma Bradbury
Caroline Rowlands

Philip Allan Updates
Market Place
Deddington
Oxfordshire
OX15 0SE

Orders

Bookpoint Ltd, 130 Milton Park, Abingdon, Oxfordshire, OX14 4SB
tel: 01235 827720
fax: 01235 400454
e-mail: uk.orders@bookpoint.co.uk
Lines are open 9.00 a.m.–5.00 p.m., Monday to Saturday, with a 24-hour message
answering service. You can also order through the Philip Allan Updates website:
www.philipallan.co.uk

ISBN 978-1-84489-507-6

Cover illustration by John Spencer
Printed in Spain

Philip Allan Updates' policy is to use papers that are natural, renewable and recyclable
products and made from wood grown in sustainable forests. The logging and
manufacturing processes are expected to conform to the environmental regulations
of the country of origin.

Contents

Introduction

About this book

Emma Bradbury and **Caroline Rowlands** are teachers at Aquinas College in Stockport, Cheshire. They have experience of teaching GCSE law, AQA and OCR AS and A2 law, and law access courses. Emma has an LLB (Hons) and a Masters degree in Law and Medicine. Caroline has completed a BA (Hons), the Common Professional Examination and the Bar Vocational Course.

This book has been written to help AQA and OCR law students prepare for their A2 examinations. The topics cover both specifications, but make sure you know which exam board you are taking and get a copy of the specification if you are unsure. Specifications can be found on the exam boards' websites.

Structure

There are 10 topics, which are split into headings marked alphabetically. Each heading is then split into numbered sections and subsections to help you revise an area of law in small sections, and yet still be able to see how it fits into the topic as a whole.

Topic summaries and tips

At the end of each topic is a summary. The summary is a good way to remind yourself of the main points of each topic, but remember that details get you the best marks in an exam.

Tips are included in the margin. These include definitions, exam advice and extra details to aid your understanding.

Cases

It is neither necessary nor feasible for you to remember all the cases you have learnt about. We have included the best-known cases, as well as some recent ones. If your teacher has given you a different case, use whichever case you understand and can remember better. Examiners do not want you to memorise a list of cases. It is much better to know a few cases with some detail than many cases with no detail. Cases can be used to explain a point that you are making in the exam.

Preparation for exams

Exam preparation should not take place in the couple of weeks leading up to the exam. Checking your notes are correct, organising your file and writing revision notes can be done in advance and throughout the course. Once you finish a module, or even one topic in a module, make exam preparations while the information is fresh in your mind. The more preparation you do in advance, the more time you will have to revise thoroughly before the exam.

Up-to-date notes

Check that your notes are accurate and up to date. You might have misheard something in a lesson or wrote something down that is incorrect. It is essential that your notes are accurate and that you understand them. The best way to check this is to read a textbook. You may have one that you use for the course, or else you can borrow one from the library. It is sometimes helpful to read other textbooks, as they give you different explanations that you may understand better. If you miss a lesson, make sure that you copy up and understand what you have missed. Don't put it off until you are on study leave, when it will be too late to discover that you have gaps in your notes or you do not understand something.

Organising your file

The organisation of your file should be an ongoing process. By spending a few minutes on it every week, you can make sure that your file is in the correct order and that you are carrying around only what you need for each lesson. One approach is to take the notes for each topic out of the file as you complete it. Either put them in a separate file at home (one for each module) or hold each topic together with a treasury tag. Make a title page for each topic, including which module it is for and a list of its contents.

Reading textbooks and articles

Reading is important in the study of law. When you finish a topic in class, read the corresponding chapter in your textbook to improve your understanding. You can also read chapters in advance if you know which topic you are about to tackle in your lessons. If you discover an important quotation or example, write it down and put it with your notes.

There are some excellent law journals available. Find out if your library subscribes to them, or else you can subscribe yourself. They include regular updates of new cases and changes in the law. If your teacher gives you newspaper articles, information from the internet or reports from law journals, summarise the important points to add to your notes.

Understanding

If you do not understand something that you study in class or read in a textbook, you must ask for help (e.g. asking one of your classmates to explain it to you in their own words or seeing your teacher after class). It is difficult to learn something and write about it in an exam if you do not really understand it. It will be obvious to an examiner if you have simply memorised information. Do not wait until just before the exam to ask for help; do it while the topic is still fresh in your mind.

Making revision notes

Revision notes can be made in advance. It is difficult to revise from long notes, so make concise points that trigger your memory. Use your class notes and textbooks to learn the law and then use short revision notes to remind you of the main points.

Revision notes should be clear and not simply a copy of your classnotes. Try to keep to one piece of A4 paper per topic. Use different coloured pens and a clear format, e.g. cases written in red pen, statutes written in green pen. Writing things down is a good way to memorise information — it is much better than simply reading it.

Revision notes should be concise. Use abbreviations and write down only the minimum amount of information necessary to trigger your memory. For example, if you are making revision notes on negligence, use 'neg'. However, remember that it may not be appropriate to abbreviate terms in an examination.

Planning for exams

Timetable

It is essential to organise your time in the run-up to the exams:

- You need to decide how much time to allocate to revising each topic. This will help you work out how much time you need and when you should start your revision programme. If your exams are in June, Easter is the best time to start.
- You should allocate yourself time each day for revising.
- Make a timetable that includes time for study as well as other activities that you do.
- Stick to the timetable. If something comes up, you need to reallocate the revision you were going to do to another time.
- Keep the sessions short, e.g. 45 minutes, and take breaks. Alternate the subjects that you are revising in a day so you do not get bogged down with too much law.

The exam

Make sure you find out the exact dates and times of the exams that you are taking. It may be that you are taking two or even three exams one after the other. Always double-check to make sure you know whether exams are in the morning or afternoon. Try to find out in advance which room the exam is going to be held in.

It is also important that you know the format of the exam. Look at past papers so that you know how many questions to answer and how much time to allocate to each question.

Revision

Past papers

Looking at past exam papers is an excellent way to prepare for the sorts of questions you will face in the exam. The exam papers offer you a choice of question. Make sure that you would be able to answer the appropriate number of questions on each past paper. There may be topics in a module that you would prefer to answer in an exam, but it is extremely risky to try to 'question-spot'. Make sure you could answer questions on topics other than your favourites, in case your favourites are not there.

Your teacher should be able to provide you with past papers, but you can also get them from the exam board websites. It is useful too to look at the mark schemes and examiner's reports (also available on the internet). The mark scheme lists the potential content that the examiner is expecting for each question on the exam paper. You can compare what you think you would write for a question with what the examiner is expecting to see. The examiner's report is written by the chief examiner and explains where candidates had weaknesses and which questions were answered well.

Techniques

There are many methods of revising and you may already know what works best for you. However, it can be worth trying other techniques. Using different coloured pens and diagrams is discussed above.

When it comes to remembering cases, either you can keep testing yourself until the information reaches your long-term memory or you can try other techniques. Perhaps you could associate the name of the case and what happened with a picture. It could even be a scene. A silly image is often easier to remember.

Some students learn best by reading out loud or hearing their notes spoken (auditory learning). You could read from your notes or revise with a classmate and explain different points to each other. You could even tape your voice and listen to it on your way to the exam.

Testing yourself

To commit information to memory, it is necessary to keep testing yourself. The repetition helps you learn facts and figures. Getting someone to test you is always a good idea, but try this with a classmate, as asking a parent to test you can often lead to arguments.

An excellent way to test yourself is by reading through your revision notes and then trying to write down the main points. You may recall only a few the first time you do it, but with practice you will remember more. The more you test yourself, the more you will remember.

Timed questions

Many students run out of time in the exam, so you need always to be aware of how long you can spend on each question. Practise exam technique by writing timed answers to past papers. Another useful exercise is to put your notes away and try to write down as much as you can remember about a topic in 10 minutes. Then look back at your notes to see what you have missed. The more you do this, the more you will remember each time.

The night before

Many people say you should not revise the night before an exam. Although you should not be writing revision notes the night before, you can always read through your notes. Double-check the time of the exam and get together the equipment you will need. Your pencil case must be see-through, but if you have not got one, just take your pens loose. Your answers should be written in blue or black ink (e.g. biro), so take a few pens in case one runs out.

Exam techniques

In the exam room

Remember that mobile phones must be switched off and must not be in your pocket or anywhere near your desk. If you have a phone on you, give it to the invigilator to look after.

Get to the exam room early so that you can find your seat number and get settled. Read the instructions on the exam paper carefully.

Planning and timing

Before answering the questions, read through the whole paper. It is worth writing a quick plan of your answer so that you structure it well and do not forget to include important information. There is no need to cross out a plan, as the examiner may like to see it.

You must be very strict with yourself about how long you spend on each question. Find out in advance how long you can spend on a question worth a certain amount of marks in the exam, e.g. if you have to answer three 20-mark questions in 1 hour, you have 20 minutes to answer each.

Your own opinion

Most exams do not require you to give your own opinion, so it is best avoided. Starting sentences with 'I think…' is not appropriate. It is likely that a judge or legal academic has already thought it before you, so it would be best to quote them instead. If you do not know who made a certain point, then start your sentence in a more general manner, e.g. 'It has also been remarked…' or 'Some may argue…'

In a problem question, it is not necessary to state what crime has definitely been committed. Instead, explain the more likely crime and remark that the final decision would be up to the jury.

Answer the question

This may seem obvious, but examiners constantly complain about candidates not answering the question. Students see a question on the exam paper and try to write everything they know in the hope that some of it will be appropriate. This is not what the examiners want. Make sure you read the question carefully and underline the important parts. An example of an exam question could be:

Discuss the current law on vicarious liability.

The important parts of this question are 'discuss', 'current' and 'vicarious liability'. The word 'discuss' indicates that this question requires an explanation of the current law and a balanced evaluation. This means that you would include both advantages and disadvantages of the current law. Always try to use cases to illustrate your point and include the suggestions for reform that have been made by the Law Commission and legal academics.

By making reference throughout your answer to the words used in the question, you are showing the examiner that you are answering the actual question and not one that you hoped would come up.

Use examples

Students who do well in law exams include examples in their answers. This could be an Act of Parliament that created a law, a statistic, a quotation by a judge, a criticism made by the Law Commission or legal academic, or a case that illustrates a point of law. Always try to use examples in your answers but do not just list cases. It is usually necessary to give a bit of detail about the facts of a case, or the law that it established, in order to illustrate a point.

Write in continuous prose

Answers to exam questions should be written as an essay with a proper structure and a conclusion. This is difficult in the time constraints of the exam, but you should try to avoid lists, bullet points and diagrams if you can. Short-answer questions should always be answered in full sentences.

Negligence was defined by Alderson LJ in *Blyth* v *Birmingham Waterworks Co.* (1856):

> Negligence is the omission to do something which a reasonable man, guided upon those considerations which ordinarily regulate the conduct of human affairs, would do, or doing something which a prudent and reasonable man would not do.

In order to establish a successful claim in the tort of negligence, the claimant has to prove that:

- the defendant owed him/her a duty of care
- there was a breach of this duty by the defendant
- this breach was the cause of harm suffered by the claimant, for which damages can be recovered from the defendant according to the remoteness of damages rule

A Duty of care

The 'neighbour principle', established by Lord Atkin in *Donoghue* v *Stevenson* (1932), was the traditional way in which a court decided if a duty of care was owed. The principle considers the question 'who in law is my neighbour?', to which Lord Atkin responded:

> ...persons who are so closely and directly affected by my act that I ought reasonably to have had them in contemplation as being so affected, when I am directing my mind to the acts or omissions which are called in question.

Donoghue v Stevenson (1932)

Donoghue suffered gastroenteritis after drinking a bottle of ginger beer that contained a dead snail. She sued Stevenson, the manufacturer of the drink. However, the drink had been bought for Donoghue by a friend, and therefore she could not make a claim under contract law. The House of Lords made a landmark decision when it determined that a duty of care was owed.

Following this case, the courts were able to decide who owed a duty of care. However, judges found themselves making policy decisions to avoid certain people owing a duty of care, even when the claimants were closely and directly affected.

> A policy decision is where a judge decides a case according to what is in the interest of the public.

The House of Lords made a policy decision when it decided that a barrister did not owe a duty of care to his client in *Rondel* v *Worsley* (1967). Barristers enjoyed this immunity until the case of *Hall* v *Simons* (2000), when the House of Lords decided it was no longer in the interests of the public for this rule to continue.

Another policy decision was made in *Hill* v *Chief Constable of West Yorkshire Police* (1988).

Hill v Chief Constable of West Yorkshire Police (1988)

The mother of a young girl who was murdered by the Yorkshire Ripper tried to sue the police. She believed that the police were responsible for her daughter's death, in that they had failed to catch the serial killer quickly enough. The House of Lords held that it was not in the interests of the public for the police to be held accountable to the families of victims for failing to prevent a crime.

This immunity that the police enjoyed was questioned in the European Court of Human Rights.

Osman v UK (2000)

The failure of the police to follow up reports of attacks on a family that resulted in the death of a man and the injury of his son was held to be a breach of Article 6 of the European Convention of Human Rights.

Z v UK (2001)

A local authority that failed to protect a child from abuse from its parents was held to breach Article 13 of the European Convention of Human Rights.

As a result of these cases, the courts will not apply blanket immunity to all police officers who are sued for negligence. Since *Brooks* v *Commissioner of the Police for the Metropolis* (2005), each new case is decided on its facts. Failure to prevent a crime will not establish a duty of care, unless the police have 'assumed a responsibility' towards that person.

Home Office v Dorset Yacht Co. Ltd (1970)

The Home Office was held responsible for the damage done by boys who were supposed to be detained by prison officers but who escaped and damaged the claimant's yachts.

Alexandrou v Oxford (1993)

The police did not owe a duty of care to a person who was burgled. Even though that person had called 999, the burglars got away.

The neighbour principle has since been modified into a three-stage test, which was defined in *Caparo Industries PLC* v *Dickman* (1990). In this modern approach, judges decide if a duty of care is owed according to an incremental list of categories of people who do or do not owe a duty of care. In this way, a judge will follow the precedent set in an earlier case, e.g. *Ross* v *Caunters* (1980) established that a solicitor does owe a duty to his clients. Other established categories include doctor and patient; and motorist and other road user. In novel situations, judges decide whether a new category should be added by analogy with existing categories.

Caparo Industries PLC v Dickman (1990)

This case laid down the three questions that must be addressed in order for a duty of care to be imposed:

- Was the damage or harm reasonably foreseeable?
- Is there sufficient proximity between the claimant and the defendant?
- Is it just, fair and reasonable to impose a duty of care?

This case involved investors trying to get compensation for shares they had bought that lost money.

1

Was the damage or harm reasonably foreseeable?

If the ordinary reasonable person could not foresee the damage to the claimant, a duty of care is not owed.

It is not necessary for you to know the facts of *Caparo Industries PLC* v *Dickman* when discussing it in terms of general negligence (the facts of this case become more important in the later topic of negligent misstatement).

This is an objective test, where the court decides liability based on the ordinary reasonable person rather than the people involved in the case.

Bourhill v *Young* (1943)

It was not foreseeable that a woman would suffer a miscarriage after hearing a motorbike accident. The defendant did not owe a duty of care to the claimant.

Maguire v *Harland and Wolff PLC* (2005)

The claimant became ill from exposure to asbestos that her husband had on his work clothes. She tried to claim compensation from his employers. This case dates back to 1965, when the dangers of asbestos were not known. It was not foreseeable that she would get ill and, therefore, her husband's employers did not owe a duty of care.

It is reasonably foreseeable that a person may try to commit suicide when he or she is in prison. Following the case of *Orange* v *Chief Constable of West Yorkshire Police* (2001), if the police follow the guidelines and believe that the prisoner will not try to commit suicide but the prisoner succeeds in doing so, they do not owe a duty of care

2 Is there sufficient proximity between the claimant and the defendant?

> Proximity is distance in time or space.

Proximity requires that the claimant and defendant have a legal connection. This link can be either a physical connection (*Donoghue* v *Stevenson*, 1932) or a relationship (*McLoughlin* v *O'Brian*, 1983).

McLoughlin v *O'Brian* (1983)

The claimant was able to claim compensation for nervous shock from the lorry driver who had caused an accident that had seriously injured her family. There was an obvious proximity between the lorry driver and the claimant's family, but the court held that there was also proximity between the lorry driver and the claimant. She had not witnessed the accident but she had seen her family at the hospital.

3 Is it just, fair and reasonable to impose a duty of care?

> Judges can misuse this part of the test to make sure that certain people do not owe a duty of care.

The courts are able to establish that a duty of care does not exist if they believe that it is not 'just, fair and reasonable' to impose a duty.

Griffiths v *Lindsay* (1998)

The court decided that it was not fair for a taxi driver to owe a duty of care to a drunk passenger who got run over as he got out of the vehicle.

Mulcahy v *Ministry of Defence* (1996)

The court decided that it was not fair for the Ministry of Defence to owe a duty of care to soldiers who are injured during a battle. This rule was extended to soldiers, who do not owe a duty of care to each other during battle.

Vowles v *Evans* (2003)

The court held that it was fair for a referee to owe a duty of care to a rugby player who was injured.

B Breach of duty

This is the fault element of negligence. For example, just because the defendant is a doctor (duty of care) and one of his/her patients has died (damage), it does not necessarily mean that he/she has been negligent. He/she must have done an act or omission that fell below the standard of care expected of him/her.

> A general standard of care creates consistent application of the rules.

The standard of care required is described as a general standard. For example, there is no requirement to reach the standard of a good driver, just that of an average driver. Breach of duty is established using the objective test, i.e. the standard of the ordinary reasonable person, or in this example, the ordinary reasonable driver.

This general standard of care was explained in *Nettleship* v *Weston* (1971).

Nettleship v *Weston* (1971)

The defendant was receiving driving lessons from her neighbour. She crashed and the claimant injured his leg. The court decided that the standard of care expected of a motorist was that of the ordinary reasonable driver, and it was assumed that such a driver would have passed his or her driving test. It did not matter that the defendant was a learner, as she had fallen below the standard of care expected.

> The standard of care expected can vary in different cases.

This general standard of care does not require the defendant to prevent harm to others in every conceivable situation.

Bradford-Smart v *West Sussex County Council* (2002)

The Court of Appeal held that the local council was not negligent when it failed to prevent a pupil from being bullied on the way to and from school. Although the school (which was run by the local council) was responsible for the safety of the pupils, this responsibility could not amount to negligence. It was decided that the school might have been able to prevent the bullying, but it was not obligated to guarantee the safety of every pupil on his/her way to or from school.

When using the objective test, the court will take certain points into account, for example:
- the defendant's age
- the defendant's profession
- characteristics of the claimant
- the magnitude of the risk (how dangerous the situation is)
- whether the defendant had taken reasonable precautions
- the benefits of the risk

1 The defendant's age

A young person does not have to reach the standard of care expected of an adult. The standard expected would be that of an ordinary reasonable person of the defendant's age.

Mullin v *Richards* (1998)

Two 15-year-old schoolgirls were having a 'sword fight' with plastic rulers. One ruler snapped, and a piece of plastic went into the claimant's eye. The defendant had not breached her duty, as nobody had realised that this behaviour was potentially dangerous.

Although the test of foreseeability in negligence is objective, the defendant was a child, so the question for the judge was not whether the actions of the defendant were such as an ordinarily prudent and reasonable adult in the defendant's situation would have realised gave rise to a risk of injury, but whether an ordinarily prudent and reasonable child of the same age as the defendant in the defendant's situation would have realised as much.

2 The defendant's profession

A doctor is expected to reach the standard of a person at his/her level in the profession. He/she would not be expected to reach the standard of a specialist when he/she is only a junior doctor. Instead, he/she would need to reach the standard of the ordinary reasonable junior doctor. This was established in *Bolam* v *Friern Hospital Management Committee* (1957).

Bolam v *Friern Hospital Management Committee* (1957)

When the court has to decide whether a doctor has been negligent, it will hear evidence from other doctors about their thoughts of what is appropriate practice. This case involved a patient being injured after having electric shock treatment without a relaxant. The court decided that this was not negligent, as it found that some doctors did use a relaxant drug while others did not.

The length of time for which a doctor has been a consultant will not affect the fact that he/she must reach the standard of care of the ordinary reasonable consultant. This was reaffirmed in *Djemal* v *Bexley Heath Health Authority* (1995).

3 Characteristics of the claimant

If the claimant is at more risk of being harmed, the defendant owes a higher standard of care to take extra precautions.

Paris v *Stepney Borough Council* (1951)

If, to the knowledge of his/her employer, an employee is suffering from a disability which, though it does not increase the risk of an accident occurring while he/she is at work, does increase the risk of serious injury if an accident should befall him/her, that special risk of injury is a relevant consideration in determining what precautions the employer should take in fulfilment of the duty to take reasonable care for the safety of each individual employee.

The claimant was employed as a fitter in the garage of the defendant borough council. He was already blind in one eye. While he was using a hammer to remove a bolt on a vehicle, a chip of metal flew off and entered his good eye, so injuring it that he became totally blind. He was able to claim compensation from his employer for not providing him with safety goggles. The defendant argued that the vehicle maintenance work that was being undertaken by the claimant was not dangerous enough to require goggles. The court decided that the defendant had fallen below the standard of care required, as it owed a higher standard to an employee who was more at risk.

4 The magnitude of the risk

If the likelihood of a risk is small, the defendant will not have breached his/her duty.

Bolton v Stone (1951)

This is a landmark case.

During a cricket match, a batsman hit a ball that struck and injured the claimant, who was standing outside the cricket ground. This was a rare occurrence and the cricket club had built a high fence to try to prevent this from happening. The court decided that the defendants were not negligent, as the likelihood of the risk was low and people cannot be expected to prevent all accidents.

Hilder v Associated Portland Cement (1961)

It was held that the defendants were negligent for allowing children to play football on their land. The claimant was injured when a football hit him, causing him to fall off his motorbike. The defendants should have taken precautions to prevent the risk to passers-by.

Chester v Afshar (2004)

This case is also considered later.

A doctor was negligent when he failed to inform a patient that there was a 1–2% risk that an operation could cause severe nerve damage. The claimant underwent the operation on her back and suffered the nerve damage, even though the doctor performed the procedure correctly.

5 The defendant had taken reasonable precautions

If the defendant tried to prevent damage or injury to others, he/she will not have breached his/her duty. In *Bolton v Stone* (1951), these precautions were the fences that were put up around the cricket ground. Such precautions are only deemed reasonable if they are considered to be common practice.

Wilson v Governors of Sacred Heart Roman Catholic Primary School (1997)

The court held that the school was not negligent when a pupil was hit in the eye by another pupil's coat on the way out of the school. It was not common practice for primary schools to supervise pupils as they left the premises at the end of the day.

Latimer v AEC Ltd (1952)

The defendants owned a factory that had been flooded by heavy rain. Oil from a cooling mixture that was pumped to machines through channels in the floor became mixed with water, and consequently the floor became slippery with oil. The defendants had covered most of the floor with sawdust. The claimant slipped on an area without sawdust, even though it was clearly marked. The defendants were not negligent, as they had taken reasonable precautions.

6 The benefits of the risk

A defendant will not be at fault if the risk that he or she took was acceptable in the circumstances.

Watt v ***Hertfordshire County Council* (1954)**
The fire brigade transported equipment on an inappropriate vehicle to save a person trapped under a car. The fire engine that should have been used was out attending another emergency. On the way to the scene of the accident, the driver of the lorry had to brake suddenly, and the equipment moved inside the lorry and injured one of the firemen. The defendant was not liable, as the risk of injury was outweighed by the need to transport the equipment.

C Damage

The final element required to prove negligence is the presence of some kind of damage, e.g. personal injury or damage to property. For example, if a motorist (duty of care) falls below the standard of care expected of the ordinary reasonable driver (breach of duty) but does no damage to anyone or anything, then he/she is not negligent.

In order to prove damage, the negligent act must have caused the damage and the type of damage must be foreseeable.

1 Causation

These are the same rules of causation as those used in criminal law.

The courts must establish that the breach of duty caused the damage. In order to do this, they use the 'but for' test. Would the claimant have suffered damage regardless of the defendant's act or omission?

Barnett v ***Chelsea and Kensington Hospital Management Committee* (1968)**
Three night watchmen became sick from drinking tea. The hospital they attended telephoned a doctor and described the symptoms. The doctor did not recognise that they had arsenic poisoning and told them to go home. Evidence showed that the doctor did not cause their deaths by not examining them, as they would have died anyway.

Thompson v ***Home Office* (2001)**
The claimant was a prisoner. He was injured by another inmate who cut him with a razor blade. The claimant failed to prove that the availability of razor blades in prison was the cause of his injury. The court held that the inmate who attacked the claimant would have found another way to inflict the injury had razor blades not been available.

In some cases, it can be difficult to establish what caused the claimant's damage.

This case involves multiple causes.

Wilsher v ***Essex Area Health Authority* (1988)**
The claimant had gone blind. Medical evidence showed that there were six possible causes of the blindness. The doctor's negligence had been only one of the possible causes, so the doctor was not negligent.

The court will sometimes allow a claim even when it cannot prove the 'but for' test of causation.

Fairchild v Glenhaven Funeral Services (2002)

The claimant's husband contracted mesothelioma (a type of cancer caused by asbestos) and died. She was unable to establish which of her husband's employers had been the cause of his illness. The court allowed her claim, as it was fair that at least one of his previous employers should be held responsible. This case allowed a claim, even though causation could not be established. It is referred to as the 'Fairchild exception'.

The issue of causation was also unimportant in the case of *Chester* v *Afshar* (2004).

Chester v Afshar (2004)

A doctor was negligent when he failed to inform a patient that there was a 1–2% risk that an operation would cause severe nerve damage. The claimant underwent the operation on her back and suffered the nerve damage, even though the doctor performed the procedure correctly. It was likely that the claimant would have consented to the operation even if she had known of the risks involved. The fact that the doctor did not mention the risk did not cause the claimant to have the operation, as she would have had it anyway.

However, the court decided that the doctor *was* negligent, as there is an overriding duty to warn patients of any potential risks. It thought that this duty to warn was more important than having to establish causation.

2 Remoteness of damage

It is not enough for a claimant to prove that *any* damage was reasonably foreseeable; he/she must prove that the *type* of damage suffered was reasonably foreseeable. This was established in the case of *The Wagon Mound* (1961).

The Wagon Mound (1961)

A negligent oil spill from the defendant's tanker floated into Sydney Harbour. Sparks from welding ignited some of the oil and it set fire to the wharf. The defendant was not liable, as this type of damage was not foreseeable.

This Australian case was decided by the Privy Council but has since been fully incorporated into the law of England and Wales.

Smith v Leech Brain and Co. Ltd (1962)

The claimant's husband was burnt on the lip owing to the defendant's negligence. The burn caused cancer and he died. The burn was foreseeable and therefore the defendant was liable for the full extent of the husband's injuries, which resulted in death.

Hughes v Lord Advocate (1963)

Post Office workers left a hole in the road unattended when they went for a tea break. They pulled tarpaulin over the entrance of the tent that covered the hole and removed the ladder. They placed several paraffin warning lamps around the hole.

The 8-year-old claimant and another 10-year-old took the ladder and went down the hole. One of the lamps was knocked down the hole, causing an explosion in which the boys were badly burned. The claimant was able to claim because, even though the explosion was not foreseeable, the type of damage (burns) was.

3 Novus actus interveniens

Sometimes, a new intervening act will break the chain of causation. This could include the unexpected actions of a third person or of the claimant. Proof of an intervening act could result in the original defendant no longer being responsible for the claimant's injuries.

Topp v *London Country Buses Ltd* (1993)

One of the defendant bus company's workers left a minibus unattended with the keys in the ignition. Joyriders stole the minibus and killed the claimant's husband when they ran him over. The bus company was not responsible for the death, as the joyriders' actions intervened and broke the chain of causation.

Baker v *Willoughby* (1970)

The claimant injured his leg in a car accident caused by the defendant's negligence. The defendant was made to compensate the claimant for his injuries. However, the claimant had to have the injured leg amputated when he was shot during an armed robbery (new act). The defendant claimed that he should no longer have to compensate the claimant for an injury to a leg that no longer existed. The court decided that it was fair for the claimant to receive compensation.

The decision in *Baker* v *Willoughby* was not followed in *Jobling* v *Associated Dairies* (1982).

Jobling v *Associated Dairies* (1982)

The House of Lords held in favour of an employer whose employee had been injured at work but then suffered an unrelated illness (new act), which prevented him from working again. The employer was liable for the injury only up until the claimant became ill.

Rahman v *Arearose Ltd and UCL Trust* (2000)

The claimant was attacked at work. He injured his eye and suffered psychiatric damage. He went to hospital where the doctor's negligence (new act) caused him to lose his eye. The employer was still responsible for the psychiatric damage caused to the claimant, as was the hospital.

4 Res ipsa loquitur

'*Res ipsa loquitur*' literally translates as 'the facts speak for themselves', and it is used when it cannot be proved exactly what happened, but the facts show that the defendant must have been negligent. This is important in medical cases where the claimant awakes from an operation during which the doctor has been negligent. The claimant cannot say for certain exactly who was to blame, as he/she was under anaesthetic.

Mahon v *Osborne* (1939)

The claimant awoke from an operation. Someone had failed to remove cotton wool swabs from her stomach, which became infected. The hospital was negligent based on this evidence.

***Scott* v *London and St Katherine's Docks* (1865)**
The claimant was hit by a falling bag of sugar in the defendant's warehouse. The fact that bags of sugar do not usually fall from the sky meant that the Court of Appeal believed there was enough evidence to find the defendant liable.

D Evaluation of negligence

1 Duty of care

Proof of a duty of care being owed is the first of three obstacles that a claimant has to overcome when trying to establish that a defendant was negligent.

The 'neighbour principle', established in *Donoghue* v *Stevenson* (1932), allowed a duty of care to be established for persons so closely and directly affected by another's acts or omissions. This means that anyone who is directly affected could potentially have a claim. It was a landmark decision in the case to establish a duty between a manufacturer and the ultimate consumer of its product (where there was no contract), and it is seen as the correct decision.

However, the 'neighbour principle' turned out to be too wide, as it established a duty of care in almost every situation. The House of Lord's response to this was to make policy decisions in order to limit duty according to what was in the interests of the public. The case of *Anns* v *Merton London Borough Council* (1978) created a two-stage test:

- First, there needs to be proximity between the claimant and defendant (similar to the 'neighbour principle').
- Second, the judge should consider whether there are any policy reasons why a duty of care should not be owed.

This use of policy decisions was criticised, as it gave judges a great deal of power to decide who should and who should not owe a duty of care. The immunity given to police (in *Hill* v *Chief Constable West Yorkshire Police,* 1988) was criticised, as were previous cases in which judges decided that barristers and judges should not owe a duty of care (*Rondel* v *Worsley*, 1969 and *Sirros* v *Moore*, 1975, respectively).

The case of *Anns* v *Merton London Borough Council* (1978) was overruled in *Murphy* v *Brentwood District Council* (1991), and the three-stage test from *Caparo Industries PLC* v *Dickman* (1990) replaced it as the test for establishing a duty of care. This was a move away from judges making policy decisions, instead establishing new categories of duty of care by analogy with existing ones. However, judges can still make policy decisions despite *Caparo Industries PLC* v *Dickman*. The third part of the three-stage test states that it must be 'just and fair' to impose a duty. If a judge does not want to impose a duty of care in a case, he/she can simply say that it would not be fair.

There are justifications for making policy decisions and, therefore, for restricting liability. It was thought that if the family of the victim of a crime were allowed to claim against the police, such actions would mean that the police would not be able to do their job properly for fear of litigation (*Hill* v *Chief Constable West Yorkshire*

Police, 1988). This immunity that the police enjoyed was questioned in the European Court of Human Rights.

Osman v *UK* (2000)

The failure of the police to follow up reports of attacks on a family, which resulted in the death of a man and the injury of his son, was held to be a breach of Article 6 of the European Convention of Human Rights.

Z v *UK* (2001)

A local authority that failed to protect a child from parental abuse was held to breach Article 13 of the European Convention of Human Rights.

As a result of these cases, the courts will not apply blanket immunity to all police who are sued for negligence. Since *Brooks* v *Commissioner of the Police for the Metropolis* (2005), each new case will be decided on its facts. Failure to prevent a crime will not establish a duty of care unless the police have 'assumed a responsibility' towards the person affected.

Home Office v *Dorset Yacht Co. Ltd* (1970)

The Home Office was held responsible for the damage done by boys who were supposed to be detained by prison officers but escaped and damaged the claimant's yachts.

By deciding that barristers could not be sued for negligence in *Rondel* v *Worsley* (1969), the court aimed to prevent people who lost their cases from blaming their barristers. The case of *Hall* v *Simons* (2000) overruled this immunity.

The issue of judges making policy decisions, for reasons such as preventing the 'floodgates' from opening, can be both justified and criticised. The issue is whether it should be up to the judges to make these rules.

2 *Breach of duty*

Breach of duty is the fault element of negligence. Most torts are strict liability, which means that there is no need to prove that the offence was anyone's fault. Negligence is, however, a fault-based tort that restricts liability. Not only does the claimant have to prove that the defendant owed a duty of care and caused damage, he/she also has to prove that the defendant fell below the standard of care expected. This adds extra burden to the claimant in proving a case. The test is objective, which means that a general standard has been established, but it can lead to impossible levels of care necessary to avoid liability.

The decision in *Nettleship* v *Weston* (1971) required the defendant to reach the standard of an ordinary reasonable driver, even though she had not passed her driving test. The advantage of this general standard rule is that if the courts took into account the personal factors relating to the defendant, the test would become subjective and much harder to prove. (Subjective tests are used in criminal law, where it is more important to make sure that the defendant is personally responsible, as he/she may face a prison sentence.)

The courts have made it difficult to prove negligence in medical cases and have been criticised for protecting doctors from liability. In order to establish fault in medical cases, the claimant must prove that a doctor has been negligent. Naturally, this makes doctors and their employers keen to prove that they were not at fault. Medical cases in particular are difficult to prove, as the medical profession may be seen to 'close ranks'. If the doctor can show that another doctor might have acted as he/she did, the courts are reluctant to find that the doctor was at fault. This happened in *Bolam* v *Friern Hospital Management Committee* (1957). Such cases rest on the testimony of expert witnesses who say that they would or would not have done the same. This makes it extremely difficult to win a case of medical negligence.

However, since the case of *Bolitho* v *City and Hackney Health Authority* (1997), the House of Lords stated that the evidence of the expert doctor would not always prove that the defendant doctor was not at fault. The court must decide if the evidence of the expert is reasonable after weighing up the risks and benefits. In *Marriott* v *West Midlands Regional Health Authority* (1999), the Court of Appeal found that a doctor was negligent regardless of expert evidence that said otherwise.

Fault-based negligence was necessary when people had to pay compensation out of their own money. These days, however, the majority of claims are made against insurance policies. The money used to pay for expensive lawyers and court cases arguing over the issue of fault can cost more than the compensation being claimed.

In 1978, the Pearson Committee suggested that there should be a no-fault system of negligence for personal injury claims. This could also be used in motor accidents, where everyone could be compensated by their own insurance rather than having to prove who was at fault. The concern with introducing such a scheme is the possibility that insurance premiums would rise and that lawyers would have less work.

In 2002 and 2003, the government made plans for legislation which would mean that fault does not need to be proved in medical cases involving babies born with brain damage. It is extremely difficult to decide whether the doctor caused the damage during the birth or if it was brought about by natural causes. The NHS redress scheme would offer up to £30,000 compensation in negligence cases, without the need to go to court and prove fault. There would also be £100,000 per year available for babies severely brain-damaged at birth. This scheme would reduce the number of cases of medical negligence going to court and, therefore, the amount of money that the NHS spends on legal fees.

3 *Damage*

The final requirement of causation — that the type of damage is foreseeable — further limits liability. The courts are extremely keen to be able to draw the line somewhere in a case to prevent a defendant being liable for everything that could possibly happen. The 'thin-skull rule' in causation means that the claimant is fully compensated, and the concept of *res ipsa loquitur* means that a claim can still be made even when it is difficult to prove who was to blame. These two principles make it easier for the claimant to succeed in his/her claim, yet the requirement that the type of damage is foreseeable from the case of *The Wagon Mound* (1961) restricts what can be claimed for.

E Areas of restricted liability

The law of negligence usually involves claims for personal injury or damage to property. There are, however, two types of claim that the courts have been reluctant to allow:

- claims for psychiatric injury/nervous shock
- claims for pure economic loss

Such claims require the claimant to prove more than the normal test for a duty of care. A defendant will not always be liable for such claims, unless the extra requirements have been proved. The main reason why the courts restrict liability in these two types of claims is known as the 'floodgates argument'. The courts are concerned that if they allow such claims to proceed, they will be inundated (flooded) with cases.

> The 'floodgates argument' is when the court does not allow a claim in order to prevent the courts being flooded with similar cases.

1 *Psychiatric injury/nervous shock*

Psychiatric injury or nervous shock is an area of restricted liability. The courts are reluctant to allow lots of people to claim when they witness an accident and suffer from some sort of mental disorder afterwards. Claimants are more likely to succeed in their claim for nervous shock if they are primary victims (they fear for their own safety) than if they are secondary victims (they fear for the safety of others). The most usual example to explain the difference between a primary and secondary victim is that of a car accident. If a defendant negligently crashes his/her car, a primary victim will be one that suffers nervous shock after fearing that he/she was going to be injured in the crash. A secondary victim is a rescuer or bystander who is not in danger personally but who suffers nervous shock from witnessing the incident. However, both primary and secondary victims must prove that they are suffering from a medically recognised psychiatric injury or illness.

The definition of nervous shock has often been discussed by the courts. In *Tredget* v *Bexley Health Authority* (1994), profound grief after the death of the claimants' baby as a result of medical negligence was considered to be nervous shock, as was pathological grief disorder in the case of *Vernon* v *Bosley* (1997). Lord Steyn said in *White and Others* v *Chief Constable of South Yorkshire* (1999): 'Only recognisable psychiatric harm ranks for consideration. Where the line is to be drawn is a matter for expert psychiatric evidence.'

> This is the definition of nervous shock.

Since the case of *White and Others* v *Chief Constable of South Yorkshire* (1999), the House of Lords has established three categories of claimants for nervous shock:

- victims with physical injury and nervous shock
- primary victims
- secondary victims

1.1 Victims with physical injury and nervous shock

This type of victim can automatically claim for nervous shock along with their physical injury. There are no restrictions placed on this type of claim and the normal rules of negligence apply.

1.2 Primary victims

Primary victims fear for their own safety and can claim if they suffer from a medically recognised psychiatric condition, and if the physical or psychiatric harm sustained was foreseeable.

Dulieu v *White and Sons* (1901)

The claimant was working behind the bar in a public house when a horse and cart crashed into the bar. The claimant was not physically injured but her claim for nervous shock was successful as it was foreseeable that harm could occur.

Page v *Smith* (1995)

The claimant was involved in a car accident caused by the defendant's negligence. The claimant was not physically injured but the shock aggravated an existing illness (chronic fatigue syndrome, ME). His claim was successful. The court stated that a primary victim would be successful in his/her claim if physical injury were foreseeable. As physical injury is foreseeable in a car accident, the claimant was able to claim for the full extent of his injuries. Lord Lloyd explained that the thin-skull rule would apply in such cases (i.e. defendants must take their victims as they find them).

This is an important case, as it clarifies many legal points regarding primary and secondary victims.

Page v *Smith* also highlights another difference between primary and secondary victims. The test for foreseeability for primary victims requires that it is foreseeable that the victim would suffer a nervous shock. Secondary victims, however, can claim only if it is foreseeable that a person of normal fortitude would suffer nervous shock.

The law regarding rescuers who suffer nervous shock while helping at the scene of an accident allows a claim if the claimant was in personal danger.

Chadwick v *British Transport Commission* (1967)

The claimant helped rescue people involved in the Lewisham train disaster. His claim for nervous shock was successful, as risk of injury was foreseeable to the rescuers. The court was also keen to show its support of people who voluntarily help out at an accident scene, so that subsequent rescuers would not be deterred from helping in the future.

In *Hale* v *London Underground* (1992), a fireman successfully claimed for post-traumatic stress disorder after his involvement in the rescue operation during the fire at King's Cross Station.

The position of professional rescuers, such as members of the police force, fire brigade and ambulance service, has been widely discussed in the case of *White and Others* v *Chief Constable of South Yorkshire*. The rescuer must be in danger personally in order to claim for nervous shock.

Since *White and Others* v *Chief Constable of South Yorkshire* (1999), rescuers who were not in any personal danger are to be treated no differently from secondary victims.

White and Others v *Chief Constable of South Yorkshire* (1999)

The claimants were policemen who were involved in the Hillsborough disaster, in which 95 football supporters were crushed to death at a football match. The policemen took part in the attempted rescue, resuscitation and removal of the dead and seriously injured. They suffered post-traumatic stress disorder as a result. The House of Lords did not allow their claims, as none of them was exposed to danger during the incident.

McFarlane v EE Caledonia Ltd (1994)

An oilrig exploded. The claimant witnessed the explosion and helped some of the wounded. His claim was unsuccessful, as the court believed that he was not in any danger himself and was merely a bystander.

Bystanders cannot claim as primary victims, rescuers or secondary victims unless 'the circumstances of a catastrophe occurring very close to him were particularly horrific' (Lord Keith in *Alcock* v *Chief Constable of South Yorkshire*, 1991).

1.3 Secondary victims

Secondary victims fear for others. They are not in any physical danger, and the court is therefore more reluctant to allow their claims for nervous shock. Certain claims are prevented owing to the 'control mechanisms' established in *Alcock* v *Chief Constable of South Yorkshire* (1991).

Alcock v *Chief Constable of South Yorkshire* (1991)

This case also involved the Hillsborough disaster. The 16 claimants were friends or relatives of primary victims and suffered nervous shock in different ways. Some were at the football ground, some were watching the events unfold live on the television and some had to identify bodies at the mortuary. The House of Lords rejected their claims and established a test for secondary victims:

- The nervous shock must have been caused by the secondary victim hearing or seeing the accident itself or the immediate aftermath.
- The secondary victim must have been present at the event or have witnessed it immediately afterwards.
- The secondary victim must have close ties of love and affection with the primary victim.

The first point of the Alcock test requires that the secondary victim witnessed the accident with his/her 'unaided senses'. Watching a disaster on television or being told about it by someone else is not sufficient.

The second point of the Alcock test requires that the claimant witnessed the event or its immediate aftermath. The definition of 'immediate aftermath' does extend to seeing loved ones at the hospital, 'so long as he remained in the state produced by the accident up to and including immediate post-accident treatment' (Deane J in *Jaensch* v *Coffey*, 1984).

McLoughlin v O'Brian (1982)

The claimant's family was involved in a car accident. She found out about the accident 2 hours after it happened and saw her family at the hospital. They had not been cleaned up after the accident and were badly injured. One of the children had died. The claim for nervous shock was successful, as the House of Lords believed that the claimant had witnessed the immediate aftermath of the accident.

The third requirement of the Alcock test is that there is a close tie of love and affection between the claimant and the primary victim. The court will assume a tie between husband and wife, as well as parent and child. The claimant will be required to prove close ties in cases involving other relatives and friends.

> This case establishes the test for secondary victims.

1.4 Evaluation of nervous shock

The main reason for restricting liability for claims of nervous shock is according to policy. The current law distinguishes between primary and secondary victims, as it is conceivable that people who fear for their own safety are a more foreseeable category of claimant. The rules governing secondary victims (including rescuers and by-standers) have become much more difficult to prove since the case of *Alcock* v *Chief Constable of South Yorkshire* (1991). The courts seem more concerned with preventing the 'floodgates' from opening than with compensating foreseeable claimants.

1.4a Medically recognised psychological condition

First, a claimant must prove that he/she has a medically recognised psychological condition. This requires an expert witness to convince the judge that the claimant has suffered more than just grief. This rule is constantly changing, with the courts allowing certain conditions and not others. In *Tredget* v *Bexley Health Authority* (1994), profound grief after the death of the claimants' baby as a result of medical negligence was considered to be nervous shock, as was pathological grief disorder in the case of *Vernon* v *Bosley* (1997). Lord Steyn said in *White and Others* v *Chief Constable of South Yorkshire* (1999): 'Only recognisable psychiatric harm ranks for consideration. Where the line is to be drawn is a matter for expert psychiatric evidence.' This means there is no definition of exactly what will be regarded as nervous shock. In *Reilly* v *Merseyside Regional Health Authority* (1994), a couple became trapped in a lift, but their subsequent insomnia and claustrophobia were not classed as nervous shock.

As medical knowledge improves, so do the categories of nervous shock. Conditions such as post-traumatic stress disorder are now being recognised, which means that the law in this area continues to develop.

1.4b Rescuers

Rescuers used to be a special category of claim until the case of *White and Others* v *Chief Constable of South Yorkshire* (1999) made them no different from bystanders. Bystanders are expected to satisfy the secondary victim test, and consequently if a rescuer does not have close ties of love and affection with the people he/she is rescuing, his/her claim will fail. The only way for a rescuer to succeed in a claim for nervous shock would be for him/her to be in personal danger and, therefore, classed as a primary victim. Two of the House of Lords judges in *White and Others* v *Chief Constable of South Yorkshire* dissented. Lord Goff and Lord Griffiths both thought it unfair to treat rescuers in the same way as bystanders. Lord Goff said it would not be fair to compensate only a rescuer who was in personal danger rather than a rescuer who saw just as many horrific sights but was unlikely to get hurt.

1.4c Secondary victims

There must be 'close ties of love and affection' between a primary victim and the secondary victim who is making a claim — just the fact that they are related does not automatically prove this test. The claimant will have to convince the court that he/she and the primary victim were 'close in care'. However, it can seem unfair that a claimant must prove during a trial that he/she was close to a member of his/her family. Furthermore, this rule does not extend to friends or work colleagues, although it is foreseeable that witnessing harm to such people could result in nervous shock.

The requirement that the accident itself or the immediate aftermath must be witnessed by the unaided senses was added to prevent people watching events unfold on television from being able to make a claim. The courts were concerned about the floodgates being opened if they allowed such claims to succeed. The 'unaided senses' rule has since been criticised, as it is foreseeable that someone who hears about an accident could suffer nervous shock.

The courts are also keen to prevent claims from people who were not shocked immediately. However, it does seem foreseeable that nervous shock that develops gradually is just as serious as if it were caused by a sudden shock.

The notion of 'immediate aftermath' has been extended in *McLoughlin* v *O'Brian* (1982) to include seeing family members at the hospital. This would seem unfair, since the claimants in *Alcock* v *Chief Constable of South Yorkshire* (1991) were not allowed to claim, even though they witnessed the Hillsborough disaster live on television.

In 1998, the Law Commission recommended changes to the current law. It wanted to remove several requirements:
- that there must be close ties of love and affection between the primary victim and the secondary victim who is trying to claim
- that the accident has to be witnessed by the secondary victim's unaided senses
- that the nervous shock has to be caused by sudden trauma

The Law Commission further argued that the current rule on compensating secondary victims is too restrictive.

2 *Pure economic loss*

The courts are reluctant to allow a claim in negligence for loss that is purely economic, i.e. the claimant has lost money but not as a result of personal injury or damage to property. Such claims are more suited to an action in contract law, and the courts also rely heavily on the floodgates argument when preventing a claim.

Pure economic loss involves money that cannot be directly attributable to the defendant's negligence. In cases involving businesses, this is usually in the form of profits which the company has to speculate that it would have made. The best case to explain the difference is *Spartan Steel and Alloys Ltd* v *Martin and Co. Ltd* (1973) (see 2.2 below).

The speculation of money that the claimant may or may not have received if the negligence had not occurred is difficult to quantify. Cardozo CJ in *Ultramares Corporation* v *Touche* (1931) called it 'liability to an indeterminate amount for an indeterminate time to an indeterminate class'.

Economic loss that is directly linked to physical injury or damage to property is recoverable. *Pure* financial loss was limited to where there was a contract between the defendant and the claimant, although after *Hedley Byrne and Co. Ltd* v *Heller and Partners* (1963), it was thought that there were some instances in which liability would be justified *without* a contract.

There are two ways in which pure economic loss can arise:
- by negligent misstatement
- by a negligent act

2.1 Negligent misstatement

Negligent misstatement allows liability for advice that was negligently given and resulted in the claimant losing money. Such liability was not allowed until the landmark case of *Hedley Byrne and Co. Ltd* v *Heller and Partners* (1964), when the House of Lords held that a duty of care could arise for some negligent misstatements.

Hedley Byrne and Co. Ltd v *Heller and Partners* (1964)

Hedley Byrne was an advertising agency that was asked to buy advertising space for Easipower Ltd. Before it did, it asked its bank (N&P) to check that Easipower was creditworthy. N&P asked Heller (Easipower's bank), which said that Easipower was 'trustworthy' up to £100,000 per year.

Hedley Byrne bought the advertising space for Easipower, but before Easipower paid, it went into liquidation. Hedley Byrne lost £17,000 and sued Heller for giving bad advice. However, Heller was not held liable because it had specifically said that its statements were made 'without responsibility', but the House of Lords used the opportunity to create a test known as the 'Hedley Byrne principle'. This test decides the circumstances in which a duty of care is owed for negligent misstatement:
- There was a special relationship between the defendant and the claimant.
- The claimant relied on the defendant's advice.
- It was reasonable to rely on the advice.

There was no 'special relationship' in *Caparo Industries PLC* v *Dickman* (1990).

Caparo Industries PLC v *Dickman* (1990)

The defendants were accountants who undertook an annual audit of a company that they worked for. The results of the audit were negligent in that they made the company look as though it was doing much better than it was. The claimants read the audit report, and relying on the favourable information, bought shares in the company. When the claimants lost money on their shares, they sued the accountants who produced the audit report.

The accountants were not liable for the claimant's losses, as they did not have actual knowledge of who would rely on the advice and how they would rely on the advice.

If the court believes that the defendant assumed responsibility, there will be a special relationship.

Usually, the court requires that the person giving the advice has some sort of qualification, such as an accountant or a solicitor. In *Chaudry* v *Prabhakar* (1988), the claimant successfully claimed from a friend who had advised her when buying a second-hand car. The advice was wrong and the claimant lost money on the car she was advised to buy.

Henderson v *Merrett Syndicates Ltd* (1994)

Lloyd's insurance made massive losses to its unlimited liability investors known as the 'Lloyd's Names'. Five of the 'Names' sued the underwriting agents who dealt with their investments. They were too late to sue for breach of contract, but the House of Lords allowed a claim for pure economic loss for negligent misstatement caused by the negligent advice. The House of Lords thought that the underwriters should have taken more care when explaining the extremely risky nature of investing in an unlimited company.

The House of Lords held that liability could arise where there is a contractual relationship, but this does not exclude a remedy in tort.

The House of Lords held that sometimes an employer owes a duty of care for an employee's reference (even when a claim for defamation was not allowed).

This case involved an employer's reference.

Spring v Guardian Assurance PLC (1994)

The claimant was a sacked employee who was given a reference that included the words 'incompetent and dishonest'. He did not get the new job he was applying for. The House of Lords allowed the claim, maintaining that because of the facts the previous employer owed a duty of care.

The *White* v *Jones* (1995) decision is an exception to the normal rules regarding pure economic loss. This case is said to extend the Hedley Byrne principle.

White v Jones (1995)

Two daughters were taken out of their father's will following an argument. When they later made up, the father instructed his solicitor to put them back in the will and to allocate £9,000 to each daughter. However, the father died before the solicitor changed the will.

This case opened up liability, but because the two cases are specific to their facts, distinctions have been made in more recent solicitor–client cases.

The House of Lords held that a claim for pure economic loss was allowed for a failure to act. It relied upon the decision in *Ross* v *Caunters* (1990), in which a will was written wrongly and did not comply with probate laws. Therefore, it allowed a duty of care using the neighbour principle in *Donoghue* v *Stevenson* (1932), without the restrictions imposed by the Hedley Byrne principle.

2.2 Negligent act

The law of negligence allows claims to compensate for the defendant's negligent act where it has caused quantifiable loss. The courts will not allow the claimant to claim for any losses that are not directly connected to the negligent act.

Spartan Steel and Alloys Ltd v Martin and Co. Ltd (1973)

The defendant negligently disconnected the power supply to the claimant's metal smelting company. The claimant claimed for:
- the damage to the metal that was being smelted at the time of the power cut
- the profits that the company was going to make from selling that metal
- future profits that may have been made during the time it took for the power to be restored and the vat mended

By limiting the responsibility of the defendant, the claimant cannot not claim speculated profits (the 'floodgates' argument').

Lord Denning allowed the claim for the first two points only. The third point concerns pure economic loss, which is not consequential to the original negligent act. Lord Denning explained his decision:

> I think the question of recovering economic loss is one of policy. Whenever the courts draw a line to mark out the bounds of duty, they do it as a matter of policy so as to limit the responsibility of the defendant.

Economic loss that is linked to a negligent act that causes damage *can* be claimed. For a short time, the law extended this to situations in which there was no damage. Both *Anns* v *Merton London Borough Council* (1978) and *Junior Books* v *Veitchi Co. Ltd* (1983) involved successful claims for economic loss where there was no damage (defective foundations in *Anns* v *Merton London Borough Council*, and a defective floor in *Junior Books* v *Veitchi Co. Ltd*). The House of Lords has since returned to the original requirement of actual physical damage in the case of *Murphy* v *Brentwood District Council* (1990), which overruled the decision in *Anns* v *Merton London*

Murphy v *Brentwood District Council* (1990) is a leading case.

Borough Council and stated that in order to be successful in the law of negligence, cases of economic loss caused by a negligent act require damage. If there is no damage, then such claims are allowed only in the law of contract.

2.3 Evaluation of pure economic loss

By trying to limit liability and prevent the 'floodgates' from opening, the courts have made the law regarding economic loss complicated.

It could be argued that the decision in *Spartan Steel and Alloys Ltd* v *Martin and Co. Ltd* (1973) was unfair. It is foreseeable that the factory would lose money while its machinery was being mended, but Lord Denning did not think that this was directly consequential to the original negligent act.

The law of tort and the law of contract have traditionally been separate, but the decision in *Henderson* v *Merrett Syndicates Ltd* (1994) allows for a remedy in negligence even when a contractual remedy is available. This means that the defendant can choose between the two areas of law when making a claim, and that the contractual limitation period for making a claim can no longer prevent the claimant later seeking a remedy in negligence. It also means that if the claimant is struggling to prove that his/her loss was caused by the defendant's breach of contract, he/she can try to claim in negligence instead.

The 'wills' cases (such as *White* v *Jones*, 1995) have provoked much criticism of the rules regarding economic loss. The claimants in these cases have not suffered actual loss, but rather they have failed to *gain* money from the wills.

Summary of Topic 1

In order to establish a successful claim in the tort of negligence, the claimant has to prove that:
- the defendant owed him/her a duty of care
- there was a breach of this duty by the defendant
- this breach was the cause of harm suffered by the claimant, for which damages can be recovered from the defendant according to the remoteness of damages rule

Duty of care

The 'neighbour principle', established by Lord Atkin in *Donoghue* v *Stevenson* (1932), was the traditional way in which the court decided if a duty of care was owed. The principle considers the question 'who in law is my neighbour?', to which Lord Atkin responded:

> ...persons who are so closely and directly affected by my act that I ought reasonably to have had them in contemplation as being so affected, when I am directing my mind to the acts or omissions which are called in question.

The modern test was defined in *Caparo Industries PLC* v *Dickman* (1990).

Was the damage reasonably foreseeable?

If the ordinary reasonable person could not foresee the damage to the defendant, a duty of care is not owed (*Bourhill* v *Young*, 1943 and *Maguire* v *Harland and Wolff PLC*, 2005).

Is there sufficient proximity between the claimant and the defendant?

Proximity requires that the claimant and defendant have a legal connection. This link can be either a physical connection (*Donoghue* v *Stevenson*, 1932) or a relationship (*McLoughlin* v *O'Brian*, 1983).

Is it just, fair and reasonable to impose a duty of care?

See *Griffiths* v *Lindsay* (1998).

Breach of duty

The standard of care required is described as a general standard. Breach of duty is established using the objective test, i.e. the standard of the ordinary reasonable person. This general standard of care was explained in *Nettleship* v *Weston* (1971)

When using the objective test, the court will take certain things into account, for example:

- the defendant's age
- the defendant's profession
- characteristics of the claimant
- how dangerous the situation is
- whether the defendant had taken reasonable precautions
- the benefits of the risk

The defendant's age

A young person will not have to reach the standard of care expected of an adult (*Mullin* v *Richards*, 1998). The standard would be of an ordinary reasonable person of the defendant's age.

The defendant's profession

A doctor is expected to reach the standard of a person at his/her level in the profession (*Bolam* v *Friern Hospital Management Committee*, 1957).

Characteristics of the claimant

If the claimant is at more risk of being harmed, the defendant owes a higher standard of care to take extra precautions (*Paris* v *Stepney Borough Council*, 1951).

The magnitude of the risk

If the likelihood of there being a risk is small, the defendant will not have breached his/her duty (*Bolton* v *Stone*, 1951).

The defendant had taken reasonable precautions

If the defendant tried to prevent damage or injury to others, he/she will not have breached his/her duty (*Latimer* v *AEC Ltd*, 1952).

The benefits of the risk

A defendant will not be at fault if the risk that he/she took was acceptable in the circumstances (*Watt* v *Hertfordshire County Council*, 1954).

Damage
Causation

The courts must establish that the breach of duty caused the damage. In order to do this, they use the 'but for' test — would the claimant have suffered damage regardless of the defendant's act or omission? (*Barnett* v *Chelsea and Kensington Hospital Management Committee*, 1968).

In some cases, it can be difficult to establish what caused the claimant's damage and there may be multiple causes (*Wilsher* v *Essex Area Health Authority*, 1988).

Remoteness of damage

The claimant must prove that the *type* of damage suffered was reasonably foreseeable (*The Wagon Mound*, 1961).

Novus actus interveniens

Sometimes, a new intervening act will break the chain of causation. Proof of an intervening act could result in the original defendant no longer being responsible for the claimant's injuries (*Topp* v *London Country Buses Ltd*, 1993).

Res ipsa loquitur

This is used when it cannot be proved exactly what happened, but the facts show the defendant must have been negligent (*Mahon* v *Osborne*, 1939).

Areas of restricted liability

The law of negligence usually involves claims for personal injury or damage to property. There are, however, two types of claim that the courts have been reluctant to allow:

- claims for psychiatric injury/nervous shock
- claims for pure economic loss

Such claims require the claimant to prove more than the normal test for a duty of care.

Psychiatric injury/nervous shock

Claimants are more likely to succeed in their claim for nervous shock if they are primary victims (they fear for their own safety) than if they are secondary victims (they fear for the safety of others). They must be suffering from a medically recognised psychiatric injury or illness.

Victims with physical injury and nervous shock

There are no restrictions placed on this type of claim and the normal rules of negligence apply.

Primary victims

Primary victims fear for their own safety and can claim if they suffer from a medically recognised psychiatric condition, and if the physical or psychiatric harm sustained was foreseeable (e.g. *Dulieu* v *White and Sons*, 1901 and *Page* v *Smith*, 1995). The law regarding rescuers who suffer nervous shock while helping at the scene of an accident allows a claim if the claimant was in personal danger (*Chadwick* v *British Transport Commission*, 1967). Since *White and Others* v *Chief Constable of South Yorkshire* (1999), rescuers who are not in personal danger are to be treated no differently from secondary victims.

Secondary victims

Secondary victims fear for others. They are not in any physical danger and the courts are therefore more reluctant to allow their claims for nervous shock. Certain claims are prevented as a result of the 'control mechanisms' established in *Alcock* v *Chief Constable of South Yorkshire* (1991):

- The nervous shock must have been caused by the secondary victim hearing or seeing the accident itself or the immediate aftermath (*McLoughlin* v *O'Brian*, 1982.

- The secondary victim must have been present at the event or witnessed it immediately afterwards.
- The secondary victim must have close ties of love and affection with the primary victim.

Evaluation of nervous shock

The main criticisms of nervous shock were addressed by the Law Commission. In 1998, it recommended changes to the current law to remove several requirements:

- that there must be close ties of love and affection between the primary victim and the secondary victim who is trying to claim
- that the accident has to be witnessed by the secondary victim's unaided senses
- that the nervous shock has to be caused by sudden trauma

The Law Commission further argued that the current rule on compensating secondary victims is too restrictive.

Pure economic loss

Pure economic loss involves money that cannot be directly attributed to the defendant's negligence. In cases involving businesses, this is usually in the form of profits which the company has to speculate that it would have made. The best case to explain the difference is *Spartan Steel and Alloys Ltd* v *Martin and Co. Ltd* (1973). Cardozo CJ in *Ultramares Corporation* v *Touche* (1931) called it 'liability to an indeterminate amount for an indeterminate time to an indeterminate class'.

Economic loss that is directly linked to physical injury or damage to property is recoverable. *Pure* financial loss was limited to cases in which there was a contract between the defendant and the claimant, although after *Hedley Byrne and Co. Ltd* v *Heller and Partners* (1963), it was thought that there were some instances in which liability would be justified *without* a contract.

There are two ways in which pure economic loss can arise:
- by negligent misstatement
- by a negligent act

Negligent misstatement

Negligent misstatement allows liability for advice that was negligently given and resulted in the claimant losing money. Such liability was not allowed until the landmark case of *Hedley Byrne and Co. Ltd* v *Heller and Partners*. The House of Lords decided the circumstances when a duty of care will be owed for negligent misstatement:

- There was a special relationship between the defendant and the claimant.
- The claimant relied on the defendant's advice.
- It was reasonable to rely on the advice.

The *White* v *Jones* (1995) decision is an exception to the normal rules regarding pure economic loss. This case is said to extend the Hedley Byrne principle.

Negligent act

The law of negligence allows claims to compensate for the defendant's negligent act where it has caused quantifiable loss. The courts will not allow the claimant to claim for any losses that are not directly connected to the negligent act (*Spartan Steel and Alloys Ltd* v *Martin and Co. Ltd*, 1973)

Evaluation of pure economic loss

The law regarding economic loss is complicated. Some believe that the decision in *Spartan Steel and Alloys Ltd* v *Martin and Co. Ltd* (1973) was unfair. The law of tort and the law of contract have traditionally been separate, but the decision in *Henderson* v *Merrett Syndicates Ltd* (1994) allows for a remedy in negligence even when a contractual remedy is available. The 'wills' cases (such as *White* v *Jones*, 1995) have caused much criticism of the rules regarding economic loss. The claimants in these cases have not suffered actual loss. Rather they have failed to *gain* money from the wills.

Vicarious liability arises when one party is responsible for the torts of another. This situation occurs most frequently when an employer is held responsible for torts committed by an employee.

The concept may appear unfair, since it holds a third party responsible for the actions of another, despite the fact that there may be no fault on the part of that third party. Vicarious liability can be justified, however, by the idea that if someone has control over another, he/she should be held responsible for the other's actions.

Employers can choose whom to employ and are expected to ensure that those they do employ are competent to perform the job. Holding employers responsible also encourages them to impose high standards in their companies. Additionally, since employers benefit from the work of their employees, some claim that it follows that they should also be held responsible for the mistakes of their employees.

Vicarious liability provides a practical way of ensuring that victims receive compensation, since employers are usually required to hold insurance. As such, they are better able to meet the cost of any claim than the employee who committed the tort. A claimant can choose whether to sue the person who committed the tort, the employer or both. In practice, he/she will usually sue the employer, since the employer is most likely to be able to afford any damages awarded.

A Key questions

In order for vicarious liability to apply, the courts must ask two questions:
- Was the person who committed the tort employed by the defendant?
- Was the tort committed in the course of that employment?

1 *Was the person who committed the tort employed by the defendant?*

1.1 Employees

Employers are liable for torts committed by their employees, but not for those committed by independent contractors. Independent contractors include, for example, plumbers or electricians hired by a householder, and they are usually responsible for their own torts.

In terms of vicarious liability, it is therefore essential to establish exactly who is classed as an 'employee'. While this may appear straightforward at first, it has proven to be surprisingly tricky in some cases, and the courts have developed several tests to determine the status of a person's employment.

1.2 Tests for status of employment

Over the years, the courts have used several different tests to try to determine whether someone can be classified as an employee. The courts do not use a single test but instead look at all the factors and circumstances before reaching a decision on employment status.

1.2a Control test

The courts look at who has control over the way in which the work is carried out. If the employer sets out how the work is to be done and when it is to be done by, the courts are more likely to consider the person carrying out the work to be an employee. If, on the other hand, it was up to the person carrying out the work to determine how and when it should be done, that person would be more likely to be classed as an independent contractor. For example, a householder who hired an electrician would be unlikely to tell him/her how to rewire the house — it is clear that the electrician would be an independent contractor.

This test was used in many of the early cases; however, if the work is especially skilled or sophisticated, the test becomes less effective. Surgeons, for example, are employed by NHS trusts. These trusts are run by managers who do not have the relevant knowledge to instruct the surgeons on how to carry out operations. Despite this, surgeons are considered to be employees. Managers in the IT industry may have limited understanding of the technology involved and would not be able to tell a computer programmer how write the required programme. However, such programmers may still be classed as employees.

1.2b Integration test

This test asks whether the person's work is an integral part of the business. A person employed to work on the till in a shop would usually be an employee; however, if the till was broken, the person called in to fix it would probably be an independent contractor, as his/her work would be incidental to the business of running the shop.

Stevenson, Jordan and Harrison Ltd v *Macdonald and Evans* (1952)
In this case, Lord Denning stated:

> Under a contract of service, a man is employed as part of a business, and his work is done as an integral part of the business; whereas under a contract for services, his work, although done for the business, is not integrated into it but is only an accessory to it.

1.2c Economic reality test

The courts may also look at any contract between the two parties, as these terms may indicate the status of the relationship. It may be a contract of service, in which case the person is more likely to be an employee, or it may be a contract for services, which would indicate an independent contractor. It would be for the court to decide based on several factors.

Ready Mixed Concrete v *Minister of Pensions and National Insurance* (1968)
Mackenna J stated that:

> A contract of service exists if these three conditions are fulfilled.
> - The servant agrees that, in consideration of a wage or other remuneration, he will provide his own work and skill in the performance of some service for his master.
> - He agrees, expressly or impliedly, that in the performance of that service he will be subject to the other's control in a sufficient degree to make that other master.
> - The other provisions of the contract are consistent with its being a contract of service.

Conditions inconsistent with a contract of service may include, for example:

These conditions all
indicate that someone
is an independent
contractor.

- the ability to hire your own employees
- the requirement that you provide your own tools and materials
- the fact that you pay your own tax and national insurance

The courts will also consider how and when someone is paid, whether it is a lump sum for a job or a monthly salary.

1.3 Employees on loan

Sometimes, an employee may be 'on loan' to another employer. If the employee commits a tort while on loan, it must be determined whom he/she was working for at the time. The usual rule is that employees remains the responsibility of the first employer who loaned them out.

Mersey Docks and Harbour Board v *Coggins and Griffith (Liverpool) Ltd* (1947)

A crane driver, along with his mobile crane, was lent out by his employer, Mersey Docks and Harbour Board, to another company. The contract between the two companies stated that the Harbour Board retained responsibility for paying and dismissing him, but that he was to be the servant of the hiring company that told him which jobs to do each day.

The claimant was injured by the negligence of the crane driver and the question arose as to whether it was the Harbour Board or the hiring company who had responsibility over the driver. The House of Lords held that although it was possible to temporarily transfer the services of an employee so that he/she becomes the responsibility of another company, it was up to the original employer to prove that this had been done. On the facts of the case, the Harbour Board had not proved that responsibility for the crane driver had been transferred and so remained liable for any torts that he committed.

2 *Was the tort committed in the course of that employment?*

An employer will only be liable for torts that an employee commits in the course of employment. This is determined on the facts of each case. This may, at first, appear to be straightforward; as long as the tort was committed when the employee was doing his/her job, the employer is liable. Problems arise, however, when an employee was doing his/her job in an unauthorised manner or in a way expressly forbidden by the employer. The courts often struggle to determine what exactly the phrase 'in the course of employment' means, and there is no definitive test.

The classic test is that of Salmond, taken from the text *Salmond on Torts*, which stated that tortious acts are done in the course of employment if they are:

- wrongful acts actually authorised by the employer, or
- wrongful and unauthorised ways of doing acts authorised by the employer

Thus, an employer will be vicariously liable for an employee's tort when:

- the employee has carried out an authorised act in a careless way
- the employer has allowed the employee to do an unlawful act

- the employee has carried out an authorised act in an unauthorised way
- the employee has carried out an act that had been expressly forbidden but was for the benefit of the employer

2.1 The employee has carried out an authorised act in a careless way

This is the classic example of vicarious liability and the most common.

Century Insurance v *Northern Ireland Road Transport Board* (1942)

An employee of the defendant company, who drove a petrol lorry for it, caused an explosion when he lit a cigarette and discarded the match while transferring petrol to an underground tank. The claimant's property was damaged and he sued the defendants. The defendants were held liable for the damage caused, as it was deemed that the driver was acting in the course of his employment — this was simply a negligent way of carrying out what he was authorised to do.

2.2 The employer has allowed the employee to do an unlawful act

It is obvious that if an employer authorises or permits an unlawful act, then it will incur liability for that act.

2.3 The employee has carried out an authorised act in an unauthorised way

The employer may be vicariously liable if the employee does an authorised act but in an unauthorised way.

Limpus v *London General Omnibus Co.* (1862)

Bus drivers were given a card stating that they 'must not on any account race with or obstruct another omnibus'. A driver employed by the defendants ignored the instructions on the card and obstructed another bus, causing an accident. The employers were vicariously liable because the damage resulted from the driver doing an authorised act — driving the bus — albeit in an unauthorised way.

Weir v *Chief Constable of Merseyside Police* (2003)

An off-duty policeman took a police van without asking, in order to help his girlfriend move house. During the move, he assaulted the claimant after complaints by the policeman's girlfriend that the claimant was rummaging through her belongings. The policeman pushed the claimant down the stairs, punched him and locked him in the police van, telling him that he was taking him to the police station. Despite the fact that he was off duty, his employers were still held to be vicariously liable for his actions as he had identified himself as a police officer, albeit one that was behaving badly.

Lister v *Hesley Hall* (2001)

The claimants were pupils at a boarding school for children with emotional and behavioural difficulties. While there, they were sexually abused by the warden. He was imprisoned and the claimants brought claims for personal injury against his employers.

The House of Lords said that the key question was whether the warden's torts were so closely connected with his employment that it would be fair and just to hold the employers vicariously liable. It decided that on the facts of the case the answer was 'yes', since the sexual abuse was 'inextricably interwoven with the carrying out by the warden of his duties'. Thus, the defendants were held to be vicariously liable.

2.4 The employee has carried out an act that had been expressly forbidden but was for the benefit of the employer

An employer may be vicariously liable for a tort committed by an employee, even if the employee's actions had been expressly forbidden.

Rose v *Plenty* (1976)

Employers placed a notice at their depot expressly forbidding their milkmen to allow children onto their vehicles. One notice stated: 'Children and young persons must not in any circumstances be employed by you in the performance of your duties.' Despite this, one milkman allowed a 13-year-old boy to help him on his round. The employers were held vicariously liable when the boy was injured as a result of the milkman's negligent driving. The Court of Appeal held that the milkman was doing the job that he had been employed to do for the benefit of the employers, and as such it was conduct which was in the course of his employment, despite the fact that he had breached the employer's express instructions.

Employers will not be liable for the actions of an employee who is on a 'frolic of his own'. This simply means that employers will not be liable for acts done by employees that are unrelated to the employment and from which they derive no benefit.

Hilton v *Thomas Burton (Rhodes) Ltd* (1961)

Four workmen took an extended break and drove in their employer's van to a café. While returning, there was an accident due to the negligence of the driver and one of the workmen was killed. His wife sued the employer.

The workmen had been allowed to use the van to travel to a demolition site, but the court had to decide whether this included driving to a café. It was held that the test to be applied was whether, at the time of the accident, the driver had been doing something that he was employed to do. The courts decided that on the facts, he was not, and instead he was on a 'frolic of his own'. Therefore, the employer was not vicariously liable for the workman's negligence.

Heasmans v *Clarity Cleaning* (1987)

A cleaner, employed by the defendant, used the claimant's phones to make long-distance calls costing almost £1,500. The Court of Appeal held that the defendant was not vicariously liable, as the calls were not made in the course of employment — the cleaner was not cleaning the phones in an unauthorised way, but using them for personal benefit.

2.5 Criminal acts

Employers will not usually be responsible for criminal acts done by their employees.

Keppel Bus Company v *Sa'ad bin Ahmad* (1974)

The claimant was a passenger on a bus who was blinded after being hit in the eye during an argument with the bus conductor. The bus company was not held vicariously liable for the conductor's actions, since he was not acting in the course of his employment — it was not part of his job to be violent to passengers.

The bus company may have been vicariously liable if the conductor had been acting in accordance with his duties, for example if he was trying to restrain the passenger to prevent trouble on the bus. This is because an employer may be held vicariously liable for an employee who carries out his/her duties in a criminal manner.

Morris v *Martin and Sons Ltd* (1966)

The claimant had sent her fur coat to a third party to be cleaned. With her permission, the third party sent it to the defendant cleaning company. The court held the company vicariously liable when its employee stole the coat.

3 Employer's indemnity

This decision has been criticised for under-mining the whole concept of vicarious liability and in practice, most insurers have a 'gentleman's agreement' not to pursue an employee for damages in these cases.

As vicarious liability means that two parties are held responsible for a tort, the **Civil Liability (Contribution) Act 1978** applies. This means that an employer found vicariously liable may, in turn, sue its employee to recover some or all of the damages awarded against it. Common law also allows the employer to recover damages from the employee in certain circumstances.

Lister v *Romford Ice and Cold Storage Co.* (1957)

Lister was a lorry driver employed by Romford Ice. In the course of his employment, he drove negligently, injuring his father who was also employed by the same company. His father sued the company, which was found vicariously liable and ordered to pay damages. In turn, the company sued the son whose negligent driving had caused his father's injuries. The company was awarded damages when the court held that the son had breached an implied term in his contract of employment that required him to take reasonable care.

4 Independent contractors

As discussed above, the general rule is that a person who employs an independent contractor will not usually be responsible for any tortious acts committed by the contractor.

Alcock v *Wraith* (1991)

Remember the tests that the courts use to determine whether someone is an employee or an independent contractor.

The claimant and the defendant lived in neighbouring terraced houses that shared a roof. The defendant employed a builder to carry out work on the roof. The claimant sued when this work damaged his section of the roof, allowing rain to enter his house. On the facts, the defendant was found liable, but the general principle was set out as follows:

> Where someone employs an independent contractor to do work on his behalf, he is not in the ordinary way responsible for any tort committed by the contractor in the course of the execution of the work.

Occasionally, however, liability may be imposed on the person who employed the independent contractor if he/she is in breach of a duty that he/she owes to the claimant, for example if the person has not checked that the independent contractor is competent to undertake the work. A breach may also occur if the duty cannot be delegated to another — commonly termed 'non-delegable'. It is a question of law in each case as to whether a duty can be delegated or not. If it cannot, although the work may be carried out by an independent contractor, responsibility for it lies with the person who employed the contractor. An example of a duty that cannot be delegated is that which falls on an employer who takes on an independent contractor to carry out work that is inherently dangerous. The employer will owe a duty to those who might be injured by such work.

Summary of Topic 2

Vicarious liability arises when one party is responsible for the torts of another, most usually when an employer is held responsible for torts committed by an employee. The concept may appear unfair but it can be justified, for example, by the idea that if someone has control over another, he/she should be held responsible for the other's actions. Vicarious liability also provides a practical way of ensuring that victims get compensation, since employers are usually required to hold insurance to meet the costs of a claim.

Key questions

In order for vicarious liability to apply, the courts must ask two questions:
- Was the person who committed the tort employed by the defendant?
- Was the tort committed in the course of that employment?

Was the person who committed the tort employed by the defendant?
Tests for status of employment
The courts do not use a single test but instead look at all the factors before reaching a decision on employment status.

The control test
The courts look at who has control over the way in which the work is carried out. If the employer sets out how the work is to be done and when it is to be done by, the courts have been more likely to consider the person carrying out the work to be an employee. This test can be useful, but if the work is especially skilled or sophisticated, the test becomes less effective.

The integration test
This test asks whether the person's work is an integral part of the business.

The economic reality test
The courts may also look at any contract between the two parties, as these terms may indicate the status of the relationship. It may be a contract of service or a contract for services. It is for the court to decide based on several factors.

Employees on loan
Sometimes, an employee may be 'on loan' to another employer. If the employee commits a tort while on loan, the usual rule is that employees remain the responsibility of the first employer who loaned them out.

Was the tort committed in the course of that employment?
An employer will only be liable for torts that an employee commits in the course of employment. This is determined on the facts of each case, and there is no definitive test. The Salmond test states that acts are done in the course of employment if they are:

- wrongful acts that are actually authorised by the employer, or
- wrongful and unauthorised ways of doing acts authorised by the employer

Thus, the employer will be vicariously liable for an employee's tort when:

- the employee has carried out an authorised act in a careless way
- the employer has allowed the employee to do an unlawful act
- the employee has carried out an authorised act in an unauthorised way
- the employee has carried out an act that had been expressly forbidden but was for the benefit of the employer

An employer will not be liable for the actions of an employee who is on a 'frolic of his own'. Employers will not usually be responsible for criminal acts done by their employees.

Employer's indemnity

As vicarious liability means that two parties are held responsible for a tort, the **Civil Liability (Contribution) Act 1978** applies. This means that an employer found vicariously liable may, in turn, sue its employee to recover some or all of the damages awarded against it, but this is rarely done in practice.

Independent contractors

The general rule is that a person who employs an independent contractor will not usually be responsible for any tortious acts committed by the contractor. Occasionally, however, liability may be imposed on the person who employed the independent contractor if he/she has not checked that the independent contractor is competent to undertake the work. A breach may also occur if the duty cannot be delegated to another — commonly termed 'non-delegable'. It is a question of law in each case as to whether a duty can be delegated or not.

Occupiers' liability concerns the duty owed by those who occupy land (and premises upon it) towards the safety of those who enter onto the land. This area of tort is similar to negligence and was originally developed through common law, although today it is governed by statute:

- The duty owed to lawful visitors or those with permission to enter onto the land is defined in the **Occupiers' Liability Act 1957**.
- The duty owed to those who enter onto land without permission (trespassers) is defined in the **Occupiers' Liability Act 1984**.

A Occupier

Neither statute defines the term 'occupier'. Instead, s.1(2) states that the common-law rules apply.

Under common law, the test as to who can be considered an occupier is one of control, i.e. someone who has some degree of control over the premises. This means that the occupier need not necessarily be the owner of the land or premises but may instead be a tenant or an independent contractor employed to carry out work. Indeed, there may be more than one occupier at the same time.

> Remember this important case: it established that there can be more than one occupier of land/ premises at the same time.

Wheat v E. Lacon and Co. (1966)

The defendant brewery company owned the 'Golfers Arms' public house and employed a manager to run it. The manager and his wife lived on the first floor of the premises and, from time to time, took in paying guests who stayed in their private living quarters.

Mr and Mrs Wheat were guests at the pub, and one night, Mr Wheat fell down the staircase in the living quarters and was killed. The cause of the fall was attributed to the fact that the handrail was too short, as it did not reach the foot of the stairs. In addition, the staircase was unlit, as an unknown person had removed the light bulb. The question was whether the brewery company owed a duty to ensure that the handrail was safe and the staircase properly lit. The company would only owe such a duty if it were considered to be the occupier. It was obviously the occupier of the public area, but the case revolved around whether it had sufficient control over the first floor. It was held by the House of Lords that it did. This case established that there could be more than one occupier of premises at any one time, and in this case, both the brewery and the managers were occupiers.

> Remember to include cases in your examination responses to improve your marks.

Harris v Birkenhead Corporation (1976)

The local council had issued a compulsory purchase order on a house that allowed it to take possession 2 weeks later. The residents moved out but the premises were not secure. A child was injured after entering the unsecured house and falling out of an upstairs window. The Court of Appeal held that the council was the occupier, despite the fact that it had not yet taken possession of the premises. The council had the legal right of control and was best equipped to try to prevent such incidents.

B Premises

Occupiers of premises owe a duty. There is no definition of 'premises', but s.1(3) of the **Occupiers' Liability Act 1957** states that the term includes not only land and buildings but also fixed or moveable structures such as vessels, vehicles and aircraft.

C Visitor

The **Occupiers' Liability Act 1957** sets out the duty of care owed to visitors. A person will be classed as a visitor if he/she has permission to enter the premises. This permission may be express or implied. Anyone without permission is classed as a trespasser, and the 1957 Act will not apply. Instead, the **Occupiers' Liability Act 1984** contains the relevant provisions.

1 Express permission

A person has express permission if he/she has actively gained permission to be in a place, for example he/she has been asked to enter the premises. Permission can be withdrawn, but the person must be given a reasonable amount of time to leave the premises before he/she becomes a trespasser.

2 Implied permission

Sometimes, a person may not have express permission to be in a place but may still be classed as a visitor if the courts decide that he/she had implied permission to be there.

Permission can be implied in a number of situations. The police, fire brigade, those who need to gain access to read gas, electricity and water meters and sales people are all taken to have implied permission and are classed as visitors. Those who enter shops are taken to have permission to be there. In addition, the courts may also imply permission in certain circumstances, depending on the facts of the case.

> The decisions in such cases depend entirely on the facts, so it is difficult to state a general principle.

Lowery v *Walker* (1911)

For 35 years, people had used the defendant farmer's unfenced field as a short cut to the station. The defendant had asked them repeatedly not to do this but had taken no further action for fear that people would stop buying milk from him. He then put a wild horse in the field and the claimant was injured when the horse attacked. The courts held that despite the fact that the farmer had asked people not to use the field as a short cut, the claimant did have implied permission to be there and thus was to be classed as a visitor rather than a trespasser.

If someone claims that he/she had implied permission, the burden is upon that person to prove that this was in fact the case. Permission must be genuine; it is not enough that the occupier merely tolerates the person being there. If someone enters the occupier's premises in order to communicate with the occupier, he/she will be taken to have implied permission, unless it is clear that he/she is forbidden to enter, for example if there is a notice informing them of this. Examples include people delivering milk or post, or someone who is asking for directions.

3   Rights of way

A person exercising a right of way is not classed as a visitor and so is not covered under the 1957 Act. This is an old rule from the case of *Gautret* v *Egerton* (1867), which was confirmed in the case of *McGeown* v *Northern Ireland Housing Executive* (1994).

McGeown v Northern Ireland Housing Executive (1994)

The defendants owned a housing estate and the claimant lived in one of the terraced houses in a cul-de-sac. The claimant was injured after she tripped on a public footpath that ran between the houses. The House of Lords held that a person using a right of way is not covered by either of the Occupiers' Liability Acts, since he/she is not a visitor nor a trespasser but someone exercising a right. It is thought that otherwise too great a burden would be placed on landowners, and further difficulties would be caused by the fact that public rights of way pass over many different types of property.

D   Duty

Section 2(1) of the 1957 Act states that an occupier of premises owes a common duty of care to visitors to those premises.

Section 2(2) defines the common duty of care as:

> ...the duty to take such care as in all the circumstances of the case is reasonable to see that the visitor will be reasonably safe in using the premises for the purposes for which he is invited or permitted by the occupier to be there.

It is the visitor rather than the premises that has to be made safe. This means that there can be dangerous areas within the premises, but the occupier will have discharged his/her duty if the visitor is made safe, for example if the area is fenced off or the visitor is given adequate warning of the danger.

The standard of care expected is the same as that in ordinary negligence, so the occupier need only protect the visitor from foreseeable risks.

The Act states that this duty applies only while visitors are using the premises for the purposes for which they are invited or permitted to be there. Scrutton LJ summed this up in the case of *The Calgarth* (1927):

> When you invite a person into your house to use the stairs, you do not invite him to slide down the banisters.

This means that if the visitor does something that he/she is not invited or permitted to do, the occupier owes no duty towards him/her under the 1957 Act.

1 Children

The 1957 Act gives guidelines as to how the duty of care operates in certain situations or towards certain categories of people. Section 2(3)(a) states that an occupier 'must be prepared for children to be less careful than adults', so the premises must be reasonably safe for a child.

1.1 Allurements

A child is unlikely to appreciate risks as an adult would, and may be attracted to danger. Therefore, an occupier should guard against any kind of allurement that places a child visitor at risk of harm.

Glasgow Corporation v Taylor (1922)

A 7-year-old child was attracted to the poisonous berries on one of the bushes in the park controlled by the defendant corporation. The bush was unfenced and there was no warning notice. The defendant was liable when the child died as a result of eating the berries, since they were an allurement. The corporation would probably not have been liable if an adult had done the same thing, but since the berries were particularly attractive to children, and the council was aware that they were poisonous, it should have removed them or secured the area.

Jolley v Sutton LBC (2000)

The defendant council owned a block of flats. In 1987, a boat was brought onto the grounds of the flats and abandoned on an area where children played. The residents of the flats complained to the council and in 1988 the council placed a sticker on the boat stating that it would be removed within 7 days unless claimed by its owner. This did not happen.

In 1989, the claimant — a 14-year-old boy — and his friend saw the boat when they were walking past the flats. In 1990, the two boys returned to the boat, planning to repair it and take it to Cornwall to sail it. While the claimant was working on the boat, it collapsed and he suffered a broken back, rendering him paralysed.

The council agreed that it should have moved the boat as it was foreseeable that children might play on it, but it argued that in this case, since the claimant was injured while repairing the boat, it was not liable. It maintained that injury occurring in this way was not foreseeable. The House of Lords disagreed — it was not necessary for the council to foresee the exact nature of the accident. It had foreseen that children might play with the boat and suffer injury, which is what happened, albeit that the claimant suffered more severe injuries than expected.

Phipps v Rochester Corporation (1955)

A 5-year-old boy fell into a trench and broke his leg after he and his 7-year-old sister trespassed on land where the defendants were building houses. Despite the fact that the defendants knew that children played in the area, they were not liable for the boy's injuries as they were entitled to assume that reasonable parents would not allow young children to play there unsupervised.

2 Persons exercising a calling

The **Occupiers' Liability Act 1957** also covers the duty owed by the occupier to those exercising a calling. Section 2(3)(b) states that:

> An occupier may expect that a person, in the exercise of his calling, will appreciate and guard against any special risks ordinarily incidental to it, so far as the occupier leaves him free to do so.

Those carrying out a trade are therefore expected to take measures to avoid the risks associated with it. For example, an occupier could expect an electrician to take precautions to avoid being electrocuted.

Roles v Nathan (1963)

Two chimney sweeps died after inhaling carbon monoxide while cleaning the flue of a boiler that was lit at the time. The occupier was not found to be liable for their deaths, as the risks involved were incidental to their trade as chimney sweeps. As such, it was up to the men to take precautions against such risks. In addition, the occupier had also warned them of the danger of working while the boiler was lit.

3 Independent contractors

Section 2(4)(b) of the 1957 Act states that:

> Where damage is caused to a visitor by a danger due to the faulty execution of any work of construction, maintenance or repair by an independent contractor employed by the occupier, the occupier is not to be treated…as answerable for the danger if in all the circumstances he had acted reasonably in entrusting the work to an independent contractor and had taken such steps (if any) as he reasonably ought in order to satisfy himself that the contractor was competent and that the work had been properly done.

The general rule is that an occupier will not be liable for the faulty work of an independent contractor, as long as it was reasonable to hire an independent contractor and the occupier had taken reasonable care to check both that the contractor was competent and that the work was done properly.

Haseldine v Daw (1941)

The occupier had clearly discharged his duty to the visitor in this case and therefore was not liable for the injuries.

The claimant was injured during a visit to a client who lived in the defendant's block of flats. His injuries were sustained when the lift malfunctioned and fell to the bottom of the shaft. The malfunction was caused by work that had been carried out by independent contractors. The defendant was not held to be liable for the claimant's injuries, as he knew little about the workings of hydraulic lifts, so it was entirely reasonable for him to employ an expert in that area. Additionally, he had used a respected company, with which he had had dealings over many years.

Woodward v Mayor of Hastings (1945)

The claimant pupil was injured after falling on a snow-covered step at a school under the control of the defendants. A cleaner had not cleared the step properly. The defendants were liable for the claimant's injuries, as no technical knowledge was required to check whether the work had been carried out properly. A quick check by the occupier would have been enough to see that the step was dangerous.

E Damage

An occupier is liable for personal injury and damage to property under the 1957 Act.

F Defences

There are several defences to a claim under the 1957 Act. Under s.2(5), *volenti* applies, as too does contributory negligence. There are also ways in which an occupier can exclude liability: warnings and modification of duty.

1 Warnings

Section 2(4)(a) of the 1957 Act states that:

> Where damage is caused to a visitor by a danger of which he had been warned by the occupier, the warning is not to be treated without more as absolving the occupier from liability, unless in all the circumstances it was enough to enable the visitor to be reasonably safe.

Thus, if an occupier gives a visitor sufficient warning of a danger so that the visitor is made reasonably safe, his/her duty is discharged. Whether a warning is sufficient is a question of fact in each case. A warning sign may be enough if it is clear, but in other circumstances a barrier may be required. Characteristics of the visitor are relevant, so a warning sign would not be sufficient to protect a child or a blind person. Nor would it be sufficient if there were no alternative; if the path to a house is dangerous but there are no other means of access, a warning notice would not be enough.

However, an occupier does not have to warn against an obvious danger.

Darby v *National Trust* (2001)
The claimant's husband was killed when he drowned while swimming in the defendant's pond. The defendant was not liable and had no duty to warn against swimming in the pond, since the risk of drowning was obvious.

If a warning is not sufficient, the occupier remains liable under the 1957 Act.

2 Modification of duty

Sometimes, an occupier may try to lessen the duty owed to visitors, for example by putting a sign on the front door stating that he/she will not be liable for any injury sustained by a visitor. The question is whether he/she is allowed to modify the duty owed. Section 2(1) of the 1957 Act states:

> An occupier of premises owes the same duty, the common duty of care, to all his visitors, except in so far as he is free to and does extend, restrict, modify or exclude his duty to any visitor or visitors by agreement or otherwise.

It appears from this that the duty *can* be modified, but this is subject to the **Unfair Contract Terms Act 1977**. Under this statute, an occupier cannot exclude liability for death or personal injury caused by negligence. In the case of property damage, for example if a person's car is scratched, liability can be excluded only if it is reasonable to do so. This is a question of fact in each case.

Summary of Topic 3

Occupiers' liability concerns the duty owed by those who occupy land (and premises upon it) towards the safety of those who enter onto the land. This area of tort is similar to negligence and was originally developed through common law, although today it is governed by statute:

- The duty owed to lawful visitors or those with permission to enter onto the land is defined in the **Occupiers' Liability Act 1957**.
- The duty owed to those who enter onto land without permission (trespassers) is defined in the **Occupiers' Liability Act 1984**.

Occupier

Neither statute defines the term 'occupier'. Instead, s.1(2) states that the common-law rules apply. Under common law, the test as to who can be considered an occupier is one of control, i.e. someone who has some degree of control over the premises. There may be more than one occupier at the same time.

Premises

Occupiers of premises owe a duty. There is no definition of 'premises', but s.1(3) of the **Occupiers' Liability Act 1957** states that the term includes not only land and buildings but also fixed or moveable structures such as vessels, vehicles and aircraft.

Visitor

The **Occupiers' Liability Act 1957** sets out the duty of care owed to visitors. A person will be classed as a visitor if he/she has permission to enter the premises. This permission may be express or implied. Anyone without permission is classed as a trespasser, and the 1957 Act will not apply. Instead, the **Occupiers' Liability Act 1984** contains the relevant provisions.

Express permission

A person has express permission if he/she has actively gained permission to be in a place. Permission can be withdrawn, but the person must be given a reasonable amount of time to leave the premises before he/she becomes a trespasser.

Implied permission

Sometimes, a person may not have express permission to be in a place but may still be classed as a visitor if the courts decide that he/she had implied permission to be there. The police, fire brigade, those who need to gain access to read gas, electricity and water meters and sales people are all taken to have implied permission and so are classed as visitors.

The courts may also imply permission in certain circumstances, depending on the facts of the case. If someone claims that he/she had implied permission, the burden is upon that person to prove that this was in fact the case.

Rights of way

A person exercising a right of way is not classed as a visitor, and so is not covered under the 1957 Act.

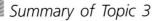

Duty

Section 2(1) of the 1957 Act states that an occupier of premises owes a common duty of care to visitors to those premises. It is the visitor rather than the premises that has to be made safe by the occupier. This means that there can be dangerous areas within the premises, but the occupier will have discharged his/her duty if the visitor is made safe, for example if the area is fenced off or the visitor is given adequate warning of the danger.

The standard of care expected is the same as that in ordinary negligence, so the occupier need only protect the visitor from foreseeable risks.

The Act states that this duty applies only while visitors are using the premises for the purposes for which they are invited or permitted to be there.

Children

The 1957 Act gives guidelines as to how the duty of care operates in certain situations or towards certain categories of people. Section 2(3)(a) states that an occupier 'must be prepared for children to be less careful than adults', so the premises must be reasonably safe for a child.

Persons exercising a calling

Those carrying out a trade are expected to take measures to avoid the risks associated with it. For example, an occupier could expect an electrician to take precautions to avoid being electrocuted.

Independent contractors

The general rule is that an occupier will not be liable for the faulty work of an independent contractor, as long as it was reasonable to hire an independent contractor and the occupier had taken reasonable care to check both that the contractor was competent and that the work was done properly.

Damage

An occupier is liable for personal injury and damage to property under the 1957 Act.

Defences

Volenti and contributory negligence apply. There are also ways in which an occupier can exclude liability: warnings and modification of duty.

Warnings

If an occupier gives a visitor sufficient warning of a danger so that the visitor is made reasonably safe, his/her duty is discharged. Whether a warning is sufficient is a question of fact in each case. However, an occupier does not have to warn against an obvious danger.

Modification of duty

Sometimes, an occupier may try to lessen the duty owed to visitors. However, the duty can only be modified subject to the **Unfair Contract Terms Act 1977**. Under this statute, an occupier cannot exclude liability for death or personal injury caused by negligence. In the case of property damage, liability can be excluded only if it is reasonable to do so. This is a question of fact in each case.

The tort of nuisance deals with the protection of an individual's right to use and enjoy his/her land. There are three types of nuisance:

- private
- public
- statutory

A Private nuisance

Private nuisance can be defined as unlawful interference with a person's use or enjoyment of land, and it usually entails civil disputes between individuals. The most common example of a nuisance claim involves a dispute between neighbours, e.g. over music being played too loudly.

In order to bring a claim, the claimant must prove:
- indirect interference with enjoyment of land
- damage to the claimant
- the interference was unreasonable

1 Interference

The interference must be indirect (e.g. noise on one piece of land which affects the people living next door) as opposed to direct interference (where the defendant has come onto the claimant's land). The interference usually needs to be continuous, rather than a one-off occurrence. Examples of interference include such things as smoke, noise and smell.

A nuisance may occur naturally if the defendant knows about it and does not take reasonable precautions.

Notice the overlap between cases of nuisance and the tort of Rylands v Fletcher (Topic 5).

Leakey v *National Trust* (1980)
The defendant owned land upon which was a naturally occurring mound. The defendant took no precautions to prevent the mound causing a landslide onto the neighbour's land and was therefore liable in nuisance.

Compare the decision in *Leakey* v *National Trust* (1980) with the case of *Holbeck Hall Hotel* v *Scarborough Borough Council* (2000).

Holbeck Hall Hotel v *Scarborough Borough Council* (2000)
The claimant's hotel was built on the council's land, and it collapsed when there was a landslide. The council had not taken reasonable precautions to prevent the landslide but it was not held liable as the damage was not foreseeable.

This is an important case in the tort of nuisance, as it made a significant change regarding the laws of who can and who cannot claim for nuisance (see page 49).

Hunter v *Canary Wharf* (1997)
Local residents who lived near the Canary Wharf building in London found that they no longer had acceptable television reception, as the building was so tall that it caused interference. The Court of Appeal decided, however, that television reception was not a right, just as people do not have the right to a view (*Bland* v *Moseley*, 1587). Therefore, the claim failed.

2 Damage

Discomfort or inconvenience will be sufficient for a claim in nuisance: there is no requirement for physical damage to have occurred. However, a claim involving physical damage is much more likely to be successful and may allow a claim which would otherwise fail.

St Helens Smelting Co. Ltd v *Tipping* (1865)

A copper-smelting factory emitted fumes that led to the formation of acid rain, which in turn caused damage to the claimant's trees and shrubs. This case would not have been successful if there had not been any physical damage, owing to the locality of the claimant's land (see below).

The normal rules of causation must be established when proving damage.

For the facts of this case, see page 60.

Cambridge Water Co. v *Eastern Counties Leather* (1994)

The damage must not be too remote and the test is based on the remoteness of damage test from the tort of negligence (*The Wagon Mound* — see page 13).

3 Unreasonable

The interference caused by the defendant must be unreasonable for a claim to succeed. This tries to balance the conflicting interests between the claimant and the defendant. Behaviour that goes beyond the normal bounds of reasonable behaviour is regarded as unreasonable.

Southwark London Borough Council v *Mills* (1999)

The claimant bought a flat in a house that had been converted by the council. She complained that she could hear the residents of the other flats and blamed the council for not making the flats soundproof. The claim failed, because it was not unreasonable for the residents of flats to be able to hear their neighbours making everyday noise.

The court will take into account:
- sensitivity
- locality
- duration
- malice

3.1 Sensitivity

The defendant will not be liable for damage that occurs as a result of the claimant's abnormal sensitivity. A claimant cannot put his/her land to an unusually delicate use and then complain when that land is adversely affected by a neighbour's activities to a greater extent than would usually be the case.

Robinson v *Kilvert* (1889)

The claimant stored paper on the ground floor of a building. In the cellar below, the defendant made cardboard boxes, which required the room to be kept warm in order to dry the glue used in the process. The heat from the cellar damaged the claimant's paper. However, as the heat from the cellar was not unreasonable and normal paper would not have been damaged, the claim failed.

If the nuisance causes general damage to the claimant's use and enjoyment of land, a claim for damage to something abnormally sensitive will be allowed.

McKinnon Industries v *Walker* (1951)

Fumes from the defendant's factory damaged the claimant's abnormally sensitive orchids. The claim, however, was successful, as there was general damage as well.

3.2 Locality

The locality of the nuisance may affect the success of a claim. People who live in the country should expect certain noises and smells, in the same way that someone who lives in the city would. For example, in an industrial area, fumes are less likely to be considered an *unreasonable* interference than in a rural area. Similarly, cockerels crowing in the morning are more likely to be considered an *unreasonable* interference in cities than in the countryside.

St Helens Smelting Co. Ltd v *Tipping* (1865)

Fumes from the defendant's smelting factory damaged the trees and shrubs on the claimant's land. Normally this case would have failed, as the claimant lived in an industrial area and should have expected such things. The defendant argued that there were many other smelting works in the area, so the nature of the locality prevented the interference from being unlawful. The claim was successful, however, as the nuisance caused material damage. The House of Lords held that discomfort to the claimant would not have given rise to a claim, but the fact that there was physical damage to property made the fumes unreasonable.

Sturges v *Bridgman* (1879)

The defendant owned a confectioner's that used machinery to manufacture its products. The claimant was a doctor's surgery that had never been affected by the noise and vibrations until an extension was built which was used as a patients' waiting room. The claimant was successful, as the locality was predominantly residential with many other doctors' surgeries. The noise from the confectioner was therefore unreasonable, although it may not have been if the area had been predominantly industrial.

The judge explained the important of locality with this quotation: 'What would be a nuisance in Belgrave Square would not necessarily be so in Bermondsey.' (These are two areas in London: Belgrave Square is a quiet residential area whereas Bermondsey is more industrial.)

3.3 Duration

The courts are more likely to consider a nuisance unreasonable if it lasts for a long time or occurs during unsociable hours.

In *Andreae* v *Selfridge* (1938), the court held that discomfort caused by temporary building work was not unreasonable unless it caused damage (as occurred in *Video London Studios* v *Keltbray Demolition*, 2001, where rubble caused damage to electrical equipment).

Sometimes, the courts have held that one-off incidents are a nuisance if they cause damage.

> A nuisance claim is more likely to be successful if there is damage to property.

> This is a leading case on both locality and the defence of prescription.

***Crown River Cruises Ltd v Kimbolton Fireworks Ltd* (1996)**
A firework display lasting only 20 minutes was considered a nuisance when sparks set fire to a barge.

3.4 Malice

If a nuisance is caused for malicious reasons, the claim is more likely to succeed. The malice of the claimant will also be taken into consideration by the court and may affect his/her chances of success.

***Christie v Davey* (1893)**
The claimant gave music lessons and often had musical parties at his house. The defendant lived in the adjoining semi-detached property and would deliberately bang on the wall, shout and scream in order to interrupt them. The claimant got an injunction to stop the defendant making such noises.

If the defendant had made a claim against the music teacher instead of making deliberate noises, he might have had an injunction granted to limit the parties.

***Hollywood Silver Fox Farm Ltd v Emmett* (1936)**
The claimant bred silver foxes for their fur. The defendant owned neighbouring land and deliberately fired shotguns close to the claimant's land in order to scare the female foxes and prevent them from breeding. The court decided that the defendant's malicious intention meant that there was a claim for nuisance and the claimant was awarded damages and an injunction.

> The outcome of both these cases might have been different if the defendants had made a claim in nuisance against their neighbours instead of trying deliberately to annoy them.

2 Who can be sued and who can sue

The most common nuisance claims concern disputes between people living on adjoining land. It is possible for there to be situations in which the creator of the nuisance (potential defendant) and the person affected by the nuisance (potential claimant) are not the owners of the land.

2.1 Defendants

In a claim of nuisance there may be a choice of whom to sue. A potential defendant could be:
- the creator of the nuisance
- the occupier of the land from which the nuisance originates
- the owner of the land from which the nuisance originates

2.1a Creator of the nuisance

It may be possible to sue the person who creates a nuisance, even if he/she does not own the land.

***Thomas v National Union of Mineworkers* (1985)**
It was held that striking miners could be liable in private nuisance when they picketed in the road outside a factory.

***Southport Corporation v Esso Petroleum Co. Ltd* (1953)**
It was held that a defendant did not have to own or occupy the land from which the nuisance originated. In this case, the defendant's oil tanker caused a nuisance when it leaked oil onto the beaches of Southport.

2.1b Occupier of the land from which the nuisance originates

It is possible to sue the occupier of the land from where the nuisance originates, even if that person is not the owner. The occupier is also liable for nuisance created by his/her employees; however, there may be an exception if the nuisance was created by an independent contractor.

Occupiers may also be liable for nuisance created by a third party or a previous occupier.

Sedleigh-Denfield v *O'Callaghan* (1940)

The defendants were aware that there was a pipe on their land which had been laid by a trespasser. When the pipe became blocked 3 years later, it flooded the claimant's land. The defendants were liable for the nuisance because they knew about the pipe. It did not matter that the pipe had been laid without their permission by someone else.

Leakey v *National Trust* (1980)

A hill on the defendants' land slipped onto the claimant's land as a result of heavy rainfall. The defendants were liable as they knew that there was a risk of this happening but did nothing to prevent it.

2.1c Owner of the land from which the nuisance originates

The usual defendant in a nuisance case is the occupier of the land, but there are situations in which the owner of the land (landlord) which is occupied by others (tenants) will be liable, for example if the owner has authorised the nuisance.

Tetley v *Chitty* (1986)

The council allowed a go-cart club to use some of its land. The noise created by the go-carts caused a nuisance to residents living nearby. The council was sued by the residents, as it must have known that by allowing the club to use the land, it could create a nuisance. The council had therefore permitted the nuisance and was liable for it.

A landlord may be liable for a nuisance if he/she has failed to deal with it effectively.

Page Motors Ltd v *Epsom and Ewell Council* (1982)

The claimant's business was disrupted by travellers who camped on council land close by. The council failed to stop the nuisance and was therefore liable for it.

Lippiatt v *South Gloucestershire Council* (1999)

Travellers camping on council land without permission to do so caused a nuisance to the claimant's farm. The council was held to have authorised the nuisance, as it did nothing to prevent it.

Smith v *Scott* (1973)

The council rented one of its properties to a homeless family. Part of the tenancy agreement was that the family would not create a nuisance. When the family disturbed its neighbours, the council was not responsible because of this clause.

2.2 Claimants

Originally, only a person with an interest in the land (e.g. the owner or occupier) could make a claim. This meant that the claimant in the case of *Malone* v *Laskey* (1907) was unable to claim in nuisance, as she did not own the house (her husband did). This law changed in the case of *Khoransandjian* v *Bush* (1994), in which the claimant was a 16-year-old girl who lived with her parents. She was able to claim in nuisance when she received persistent phone calls and harassment from the defendant.

However, the law reverted back to the original rule from *Malone* v *Laskey* in the case of *Hunter* v *Canary Wharf Ltd and London Docklands Development Corporation* (1995).

Hunter v *Canary Wharf Ltd and London Docklands Development Corporation* (1995)

The Court of Appeal allowed claims to be made by people who did not have an interest in the land affected by the building of the Canary Wharf by following the decision in *Khoransandjian* v *Bush* (1994). The House of Lords, however, reversed the decision and held that claims could only be made by people who owned or occupied land near Canary Wharf. This was done in order to simplify the law of nuisance and reaffirm that it is essentially a land-based tort.

Claimants must have an interest in the land.

Delaware Mansions Ltd and Another v *Westminster City Council* (2001)

Since the decision in *Hunter* v *Canary Wharf Ltd and London Docklands Development Corporation* (1995), the court has recognised that the rule it established for claimants may have some human rights implications. Article 8 of the Human Rights Act gives the right of respect for private and family life. By not allowing the claims of people such as children who are affected by a nuisance, the law may be in breach of this right.

3 Defences

The main defences available for the tort of nuisance are:
- *volenti* (coming to the nuisance)
- prescription
- statutory authority
- public utility

Other general defences include contributory negligence, act of a stranger, inevitable accident and act of God

3.1 *Volenti* (coming to the nuisance)

The defence of *volenti* (where the claimant is said to have consented to the nuisance by moving next to it) has never succeeded.

Sturges v *Bridgman* (1879)

A doctor's surgery extended its premises closer to a confectioner's that used machinery to make its products. The doctor's claim in nuisance was successful. Although the premises had moved closer to the nuisance, the doctor had not consented to it.

The facts of this case are explained in more detail on page 48.

Miller v *Jackson* (1977)

The claimants had moved to a house near to a cricket ground. They wanted an injunction because cricket balls were often hit into their garden. The Court of

Appeal would not accept the cricket ground's argument that the claimants had 'come to the nuisance' and therefore consented to it. However, Lord Denning disagreed with the majority Court of Appeal decision, as it must have been obvious to the claimants that such incidents could occur when you move next to a cricket ground.

3.2 Prescription

There will be a defence of prescription if the defendant has been causing a nuisance continuously for 20 years, during which the claimant was aware of and never complained about the nuisance.

Sturges v *Bridgman* (1879)

The defendant's noisy machinery had been in use for over 20 years but the defence of prescription failed, as it became a nuisance only when the doctor extended his surgery closer to the defendant's premises.

Miller v *Jackson* (1977)

The defence of prescription failed in this case as the cricket ground, which had been operating for over 70 years, had become a nuisance only when the claimant's house was built nearby.

3.3 Statutory authority

There will be no defence of statutory authority if the defendant could have avoided creating a nuisance by taking reasonable care.

This is the most successful defence in modern nuisance cases, as most nuisance-causing activities are regulated through Acts of Parliament.

Allen v *Gulf Oil Refining Ltd* (1981)

Parliament authorised the defendant to buy land and build an oil refinery. The court decided that by allowing this, Parliament must have expected the defendant to operate the refinery once it was built. The claim that the refinery constituted a nuisance failed because of this statutory authority.

3.4 Public utility

The court may take into account the benefit to the public provided by the creator of the nuisance when deciding an appropriate remedy.

This case is also explained above.

Miller v *Jackson* (1977)

The Court of Appeal believed that the cricket ground that was creating a nuisance to its neighbours should not be subject to an injunction as the benefit of having the ground outweighed the claimant's discomfort.

Adams v *Ursell* (1913)

A fish-and-chip shop was held to be a nuisance, but the court would not pass an injunction to close it down. The shop was of great benefit to the area where it was situated as it provided cheap food in a poor area. Instead, the court's injunction allowed the fish-and-chip shop to move to another part of the street where it would cause less of a nuisance to the neighbours.

However, public benefit will not act as a defence in nuisance.

Bellew v *Cement Co. Ltd* (1948)

The defendants owned the only cement factory in Ireland, yet it was forced to close because it was creating a nuisance. It did not matter that the factory provided many jobs and cement was in high demand.

There is no defence of care and skill in the tort of nuisance.

B Public nuisance

Public nuisance affects a group or class of people. It may constitute a criminal offence and be prosecuted by the Attorney General, or it can be a civil claim. Most public nuisance is now covered by statutory nuisance (see page 54), so common-law claims for public nuisance are rare.

Public nuisance differs from private nuisance as it can easily occur from a one-off event and is not based on land (i.e. the claimant does not require an interest in land and the nuisance itself does not need to arise from the defendant's use of land).

The definition of a public nuisance was provided by the Court of Appeal in the case of *Attorney General* v *PYA Quarries* (1957) as something that 'materially affects the reasonable comfort and convenience of a class of Her Majesty's subjects'. In this case, quarrying operations carried out by the defendants which caused vibrations and dust to affect 30 houses in the vicinity were held to be a public nuisance.

The Court of Appeal in this case did not specify how many people were necessary to constitute a 'class'. It needs to be enough people so that it would not be reasonable for one person to make the claim.

R v *Rimmington* (2005)

This House of Lords case involved a person who sent salt to a friend through the post and another person who sent hundreds of racist letters to people. Both of the convictions were quashed.

The defendant who sent salt through the post caused the postal sorting office to be evacuated, as the substance was thought to be anthrax. However, he did not have the mental requirement for a nuisance offence, as he did not know that the salt would spill out at the post office. He had sent the salt to a friend as a joke, thinking that his intended recipient would discover it.

The defendant who sent the racist letters had not caused a 'common injury' to a section of the public. This does not need to be physical injury but may simply cause suffering to the community. The House of Lords did not think that the people who received the letters suffered, even though they might have been offended.

This case overruled *R* v *Johnson* (1997). Now, when someone makes nuisance phone calls to many people, it is not regarded as a public nuisance.

1 *Special damage*

A person may wish to sue separately from the class if he/she has suffered more damage than the other people affected by the public nuisance.

Benjamin v *Storr* (1874)

The claimant owned a coffee house in Covent Garden, adjacent to which was the defendant's auctioneer's yard. Horses used for delivery of goods to the defendant often obstructed access to the local shops, and the smell of their urine was strong. The claimant suffered a loss of custom because the smell of the horses put off potential customers.

The Court of Common Pleas held that the claimant had suffered direct and substantial damage over and above that suffered by the public at large, and was therefore entitled to sue in public nuisance.

A common claim for public nuisance arises when people are affected while using the highway.

Castle v *St Augustine's Links* (1922)

The defendants owned a golf course that had a public road running through it. Golf balls hit onto the road were a public nuisance, but the claimant suffered special damage when he was hit in the face by a ball as he drove past the golf course in his taxi.

2 *Defences*

The defences that apply to private nuisance also apply to public nuisance, with the exception of prescription. In particular, statutory authority is widely used for public nuisance, as discussed above in *Allen* v *Gulf Oil Refining Ltd* (1981).

C Statutory nuisance

You will not be asked about statutory nuisances in your examination.

Statutory law governs some forms of nuisance that affect the environment. The local authority regulates such nuisances (as opposed to private individuals bringing an action) and issues abatement notices to stop the nuisance; failure to comply can result in a fine being issued by the Magistrates' Court. Statutes that cover such nuisances include the **Clean Air Act 1956**, the **Control of Pollution Act 1974** and the **Environmental Protection Act 1990**. An example of a statutory nuisance would be noisy neighbours.

D Evaluation

The tort of nuisance requires the court to balance conflicting interests: the right of the defendant to use his/her land as he/she wishes against the right of the claimant to not be disturbed. This can sometimes cause problems and injustice. There are certain cases that attract most criticism:

- *Hunter* v *Canary Wharf Ltd and London Docklands Development Corporation* (1995): this case is explained on page 51. The decision of the House of Lords has caused controversy for many reasons. First, the residents who claimed for the interference to their television reception lost their claim. The court justified its decision by using a case decided in 1587 (*Bland* v *Moseley*), which concerned a very different situation — the right to a view. The judge did not fully consider the importance of television in modern society and the fact that lack of reception could mean that the residents affected may have difficulties selling their property in the future. It would not have cost the developers of Canary Wharf too much money for them to install a television aerial for these people.

Second, the decision in this case to only allow claims from people with an interest in land has returned the law to its position in 1907 (*Malone* v *Laskey*). The House of Lords justified this decision as being necessary to make the law of nuisance more straightforward and to distinguish it from the law of negligence. However, Lord Cooke did not agree with the majority of Law Lords on this point. In his dissenting judgement, he argued that it was unjust to change the law back just to make it simpler. It could also be argued that the House of Lords limited the number of claimants to people with an interest in land in order to avoid opening the 'floodgates' for future cases — if it allowed others to claim in nuisance, the potential number of claims would 'flood' the courts and prevent other large building projects being viable. This is known as a policy decision.

- **Human rights**: the case of *Marcic* v *Thames Water Utilities Ltd* (2002) highlighted the fact that nuisance law may in fact breach the European Convention on Human Rights. This case raised Article 6 of the **Human Rights Act 1998**, which states that an authority (the defendant — Thames Water Utilities Ltd) should not act in a way that is incompatible with human rights. *Delaware Mansions Ltd and Another* v *Westminster City Council* (2001) also considered the Human Rights Act and, in particular, Article 8, which concerns the right to a private life. It was thought that the rule that only allows people with an interest in land to make a nuisance claim could breach this article.

  In the case of *Hatton* v *UK* (2001), the European Court of Human Rights decided that there was a breach of Article 8 when the claimant could not make a claim in nuisance because the **Civil Aviation Act 1982** prevented people who lived near Heathrow Airport from doing so.

Summary of Topic 4

The tort of nuisance deals with the protection of an individual's right to use and enjoy his/her land.

Private nuisance

Private nuisance can be defined as unlawful interference with a person's use or enjoyment of land, and it usually entails civil disputes between individuals. The most common example of a nuisance claim involves a dispute between neighbours, e.g. over music being played too loudly.

In order to bring a claim, the claimant must prove:
- indirect interference with enjoyment of land
- damage to the claimant
- the interference was unreasonable

Interference

The interference must be indirect and usually needs to be continuous, rather than a one-off occurrence. Examples of interference include things such as smoke, noise and smell.

A nuisance may occur naturally if the defendant knows about it and does not take reasonable precautions (*Leakey* v *National Trust*, 1980 and *Holbeck Hall Hotel* v *Scarborough Borough Council*, 2000).

In *Hunter* v *Canary Wharf* (1997), television reception was not considered a right, just as people do not have the right to a view (*Bland* v *Moseley* (1587). Therefore, the claim failed.

Damage

Discomfort or inconvenience will be sufficient for a claim in nuisance: there is no requirement for physical damage to have occurred. However, a claim involving physical damage is much more likely to be successful and may allow a claim which would otherwise fail (*St Helens Smelting Co. Ltd* v *Tipping*, 1865). The normal rules of causation must be established when proving damage (*Cambridge Water Co.* v *Eastern Counties Leather*, 1994).

Unreasonable

The interference caused by the defendant must be unreasonable for a claim to succeed (*Southwark London Borough Council* v *Mills*, 1999).

Sensitivity

The defendant will not be liable for damage that occurs as result of the claimant's abnormal sensitivity. A claimant cannot put his/her land to an unusually delicate use and then complain when that land is adversely affected by a neighbour's activities to a greater extent than would usually be the case (*Robinson* v *Kilvert*, 1889).

Locality

The locality of the nuisance may affect the success of a claim (*St Helens Smelting Co. Ltd* v *Tipping*, 1865 and *Sturges* v *Bridgman*, 1879).

Duration

The courts are more likely to consider a nuisance unreasonable if it lasts a long time or occurs during unsociable hours. However, the courts have at times held that one-off incidents are a nuisance if they cause damage (*Crown River Cruises Ltd* v *Kimbolton Fireworks Ltd*, 1996).

Malice

If a nuisance is caused for malicious reasons, the claim is more likely to succeed (*Christie* v *Davey*, 1893 and *Hollywood Silver Fox Farm Ltd* v *Emmett*, 1936).

Who can be sued and who can sue

Defendants

In a claim of nuisance, there may be a choice of whom to sue. A potential defendant could be:

- the creator of the nuisance (*Thomas* v *National Union of Mineworkers*, 1985 and *Southport Corporation* v *Esso Petroleum Co. Ltd*, 1953)
- the occupier of the land from which the nuisance originates (*Sedleigh-Denfield* v *O'Callaghan*, 1940 and *Leakey* v *National Trust*, 1980)

- the owner of the land from which the nuisance originates (*Tetley* v *Chitty*, 1986, *Page Motors Ltd* v *Epsom and Ewell Council*, 1982, *Lippiatt* v *South Gloucestershire Council*, 1999 and *Smith* v *Scott*, 1973)

Claimants

Claimants must have an interest in the land (*Hunter* v *Canary Wharf Ltd and London Docklands Development Corporation*, 1995).

Defences

Volenti *(coming to the nuisance)*

The defence of *volenti* (where the claimant is said to have consented to the nuisance by moving next to it) has never succeeded (*Sturges* v *Bridgman*, 1879).

Prescription

There will be a defence of prescription if the defendant has been causing a nuisance continuously for 20 years, during which the claimant was aware of and never complained about the nuisance (*Sturges* v *Bridgman*, 1879).

Statutory authority

This is the most successful defence in modern nuisance cases, as most nuisance-causing activities are regulated through Acts of Parliament (*Allen* v *Gulf Oil Refining Ltd*, 1981).

Public utility

Public benefit will not act as a defence in nuisance (*Bellew* v *Cement Co. Ltd*, 1948, *Miller* v *Jackson*, 1977 and *Adams* v *Ursell*, 1913).

Public nuisance

Public nuisance affects a group or class of people. It may constitute a criminal offence and be prosecuted by the Attorney General, or it can be a civil claim. The definition of a public nuisance was provided by the Court of Appeal in the case of *Attorney General* v *PYA Quarries* (1957) as something that 'materially affects the reasonable comfort and convenience of a class of Her Majesty's subjects'.

The Court of Appeal in this case did not specify how many people were necessary to constitute a 'class'. It needs to be enough people so that it would not be reasonable for one person to make the claim.

Special damage

A person may wish to sue separately from the class if he/she has suffered more damage than the other people affected by the public nuisance (*Benjamin* v *Storr*, 1874).

Defences

The defences that apply to private nuisance also apply to public nuisance, with the exception of prescription. In particular, statutory authority is a widely used defence for public nuisance (*Allen* v *Gulf Oil Refining Ltd*, 1981).

Statutory nuisance

Statutory law governs some forms of nuisance that affect the environment. The local authority regulates such nuisances.

Evaluation

- *Hunter* v *Canary Wharf Ltd and London Docklands Development Corporation* (1995): the residents who claimed for the interference to their television reception lost their claim. The decision in this case to only allow claims from people with an interest in land has returned the law to its position in 1907 (*Malone* v *Laskey*).
- Human rights: the case of *Marcic* v *Thames Water Utilities Ltd* (2002) highlighted the fact that nuisance law may in fact breach the European Convention on Human Rights. This case raised Article 6 of the **Human Rights Act 1998** that states that an authority (the defendants — Thames Water Utilities Ltd) should not act in a way that is incompatible with human rights.

  Delaware Mansions Ltd and Another v *Westminster City Council* (2001) also considered the Human Rights Act and, in particular, Article 8. In *Hatton* v *UK* (2001), the European Court of Human Rights decided that there was a breach of Article 8 when the claimant could not make a claim in nuisance because the **Civil Aviation Act 1982** prevented people who lived near Heathrow Airport from doing so.

The rule established by the House of Lords in *Rylands* v *Fletcher* (1868) is a land-based tort. It is strict liability, which means that the defendant will be liable even if he/she is not negligent or at fault. The rule was originally developed to impose liability on reservoir owners, but more recently it has been used to protect the environment.

This tort has not often been used successfully, owing to the number of elements that must be proved. In 1868, it was not possible for a claim to be made in the tort of nuisance for a one-off incident, whereas today, claimants who suffer such damage would probably make a claim under the law of nuisance or negligence. Despite this, *Rylands* v *Fletcher* survives and can be used in certain circumstances.

Rylands v *Fletcher* (1868)

The defendant mill owner wanted to build a reservoir on his land and employed independent contractors to assess the land. The contractors discovered a disused mineshaft, but believed it was filled with earth. Unknown to the defendant or the contractors, this mineshaft connected to the claimant's coalmine on neighbouring land. When the reservoir was filled, water poured down the shaft and flooded the mine. The defendant had not been negligent, as he had trusted the independent contractors, yet he was liable for the damage to the claimant's land. This case created a new area of tort.

Blackburn J defined the rule as:

> A person who, for his own purposes, brings onto land and keeps there anything likely to do mischief if it escapes, must do so at his peril, and, if he does not do so, he is *prima facie* answerable for all damage which is the natural consequence of its escape.

Lord Cairns added that the use of land has to be 'non-natural'.

A Elements of the tort

The definition created by Blackburn J and Lord Cairns requires that the defendant bring something non-natural onto his/her land, for his/her own purposes, and that 'thing' must escape, causing damage of a foreseeable kind.

1 Brings onto land

The defendant must bring something onto his/her land for his/her own purposes that does not naturally occur there.

Flooding caused by a natural accumulation of rainwater will not afford a claim (*Ellison* v *The Ministry of Defence*, 1997).

Giles v *Walker* (1890)

The seeds from thistles blew from the defendant's land onto the claimant's land. As the thistles were naturally occurring on the defendant's land, he was not liable.

Crowhurst v *Amersham Burial Board* (1878)

The defendant planted yew trees on his land. Some of the branches grew over the fence and encroached onto the claimant's land. The claimant's horse was poisoned when it ate the yew leaves. The claim was successful.

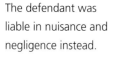

This case can be compared with *Ponting* v *Noakes* (1894), where there was no claim when the claimant's horse reached over the defendant's fence and ate the yew leaves. The claim failed, as the leaves had not 'escaped' (see point 4 below).

2 *Non-natural use of land*

Lord Cairns required the use of land to be 'non-natural'. What the courts define as 'non-natural' has been subject to change.

Rickards v *Lothian* (1913)

The defendant was liable in nuisance and negligence instead.

The outflow from a washbasin on the top floor of the premises was maliciously blocked and the tap left running, with the result that the claimant's stock on the floor below was damaged in the flood. The Court of Appeal held that the provision of a domestic water supply was an ordinary use of the land, so the claim failed.

British Celanese v *AH Hunt* (1969)

The defendant was liable in nuisance and negligence instead.

Storage of metal foil in a factory was held to be a natural use of industrial land and the claim failed. The foil escaped and hit an overhead electric cable, which caused a power cut in the claimant's factory.

These cases have made it difficult to establish that anything brought onto land in non-natural. This changed in the important House of Lords case of *Cambridge Water Co.* v *Eastern Counties Leather* (1994).

Cambridge Water Co. v *Eastern Counties Leather* (1994)

The defendants were concerned in the tanning of leather. The chemical that they used for tanning was regularly spilled on the factory floor, and over the years seeped through the ground and into the water supply. The claimant water company was unable to pump water downstream from the factory, as the pollution meant that it was unfit for human consumption. The water company sued for the money that it cost it to move its water-pumping station upstream from the factory.

The Court of Appeal decided that the damage was too remote and the claim failed. However, Lord Goff did state that the storage of chemicals on industrial land was a non-natural use.

Transco plc v *Stockport Metropolitan Borough Council* (2003)

This case considered the issue of whether water pipes are a natural use of land. The earlier case of *Collingwood* v *Home and Colonial Stores* (1936) decided that small domestic pipes were a natural use of land, whereas large water pipes were not.

In this case, a large water pipe was used to service a block of flats owned by the defendants (Stockport Council). The pipe burst and exposed gas pipes, which cost the claimants a lot of money to make safe. The House of Lords decided the defendants were not liable because the water pipe was for domestic use (servicing the 20 flats) and therefore was a natural use of land. The water did not accumulate as it was a flowing pipe and there was no escape because Transco's gas pipe was on the council's land.

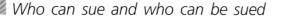

3 Likely to do mischief

'Dangerous things' include large amounts of water, fire, poisonous plants, gas and electricity.

It must be foreseeable that the thing brought onto the land is likely to do mischief if it escapes. The escape itself does not have to be foreseeable.

4 Escape

The rule in *Rylands* v *Fletcher* does not apply to things that escape from the highway onto the claimant's land (*Rigby* v *Chief Constable of Northamptonshire*, 1985).

The thing that is brought onto the defendant's land must escape from there onto other land.

Read v Lyons (1946)

This claim under the rule in *Rylands* v *Fletcher* failed because the dangerous thing did not escape. The claimant was a munitions inspector during the war and was injured in a munitions factory while it was being inspected. The court pointed out that the injury was received while in the factory and, therefore, nothing had escaped.

Viscount Simon stated that the dangerous thing must 'escape from a place where the defendant has occupation or control over land to a place which is outside his occupation or control'.

Other reasons why this claim failed include the fact that the claimant was not an occupier of land, storing munitions during wartime was a natural use of land and it was a personal injury claim.

5 Damage

Claims under *Rylands* v *Fletcher* are not actionable per se (there must be some damage).

The escape must cause damage. The normal rules of causation apply, in that the damage must be reasonably foreseeable (see *Cambridge Water* v *Eastern Counties Leather*, 1994 above).

There can be no claim under *Rylands* v *Fletcher* for personal injury. This rule was first mentioned *obiter* by the House of Lords in the case of *Read* v *Lyons* (1947). It was confirmed in *Transco plc* v *Stockport Metropolitan Borough Council* (2003).

B Who can sue and who can be sued

The rule in *Rylands* v *Fletcher* is a 'principle applicable between occupiers in respect of their land'. The claimant must therefore have some interest in the land that is affected.

Weller and Co. v Foot and Mouth Disease Research Institute (1966)

The foot-and-mouth virus escaped from the defendant's research institute. This led to a ban in the movement of livestock to prevent a spread of the disease. The claimants were cattle auctioneers who were unable to trade during the ban. Their claim for loss of income failed, as they did not own the land that was infected.

The defendant must be the occupier who is in control of the land.

Smith v *Scott* (1973)
Council tenants of a house caused massive disruption to their neighbours, who sued the council. The council was not to blame, as it was the tenants of the house who were in control of the land at the time.

C Defences

There are many defences for *Rylands* v *Fletcher*, including:
- act of a stranger
- *volenti*
- statutory authority
- default of the claimant
- act of God

1 Act of a stranger

If the escape was caused by a stranger (a third party over whom the defendant had no control), this will be a defence. In *Rickards* v *Lothian* (1913), the tap that flooded the claimant's premises was turned on by a stranger, and the Privy Council decided that this was one of the reasons why the claim failed.

Box v *Jubb* (1879)
The defendant's reservoir overflowed onto the claimant's land. The defendant was not liable because the overflow was caused by a third person who had emptied his own reservoir further up stream.

2 Volenti

'Volenti' means consent.

It is a defence if the claimant consented to the defendant bringing the dangerous thing onto his/her land. This defence will be particularly strong if the thing on the defendant's land benefits the claimant. A common benefit, (e.g. neighbours benefit from water storage on the defendant's land) means that a claim would fail if there were an escape.

3 Statutory authority

This defence requires the judge to interpret the statute.

An Act of Parliament may authorise a dangerous activity, and therefore there can be no claim under *Rylands* v *Fletcher*. Some statutes specify if the rule applies and others do not, so it is up to the judge to decide.

Green v *Chelsea Waterworks Co.* (1894)
The waterworks were under a duty authorised by Parliament to provide water. This meant that a claim for damage caused by a leak from the pipe failed, as it was foreseeable that bursts could occur.

Charing Cross Electricity Co. v Hydraulic Co. (1914)

The defendants were liable under *Rylands* v *Fletcher* when a water pipe burst. Parliament had allowed the defendant company to supply water but had not put it under a duty to do so.

4 Default of the claimant

Contributory negligence is governed by the **Law Reform (Contributory Negligence) Act 1945.**

If the escape and damage are caused completely by the default of the claimant, the defendant will not be liable. If the claimant is partly responsible, the normal rules of contributory negligence apply and the compensation will be reduced accordingly.

5 Act of God

The courts are reluctant to allow this defence unless the weather conditions are exceptional.

Extreme weather conditions may afford a defence.

Nichols v Marsland (1876)

The claimant's land was flooded after extremely heavy rainfall caused the defendant's ornamental lakes to flood.

D Evaluation

The rule in *Rylands* v *Fletcher* was established shortly after a disaster at Bradford Reservoir caused the death of 240 people. The rule was a way of imposing liability in cases involving reservoirs and had the potential to extend to other dangerous activities during the Industrial Revolution. However, the rule was established so that it was difficult to prove, and it was restricted to occupiers of land. It could have gone much further and have become a way to deter landowners from allowing dangerous things on their land to escape, thus affording protection to the environment. Instead, the subsequent cases and the many defences mean that it applies in only a small number of situations.

The House of Lords in *Transco plc* v *Stockport Metropolitan Borough Council* (2003) discussed the future of *Rylands* v *Fletcher*. The two main criticisms of the rule are:
- it is difficult to prove owing to the many elements and the numerous defences
- it is strict liability

Lord Goff in *Cambridge Water* Co. v *Eastern Counties Leather* (1994) said:

> It is more appropriate for strict liability in respect of operations of high risk to be imposed by Parliament than the courts. If such liability is imposed by statute, the relevant activities can be identified and those concerned can know where they stand.

The House of Lords in *Transco plc* v *Stockport Metropolitan Borough Council* (2003) decided that the rule in *Rylands* v *Fletcher* should remain as it had been for 150 years, and there is still a small number of cases in which the rule should be available. Lord Bingham suggested that there should be liability only where the defendant has done something where there is an 'exceptionally high risk of danger or mischief'. He also suggested that the term 'non-natural user' requires the defendant's use to be 'extraordinary and unusual'.

The Royal Commission on Civil Liability and Compensation for Personal Injury suggested that *Rylands* v *Fletcher* should be abolished, and that the government should have the power to impose strict liability on certain dangerous activities. The Law Commission suggested that the government could impose strict liability according to the concept of 'special danger', which would mean that the rule in *Rylands* v *Fletcher* would no longer be necessary. Some dangerous activities are already governed by Parliament. The **Consumer Protection Act 1987** governs defective products. It also imposes strict liability, as does the **Environmental Protection Act 1990** and other EU laws regarding health and safety.

Summary of Topic 5

In *Rylands* v *Fletcher* (1868), the defendant mill owner wanted to build a reservoir on his land and employed independent contractors to assess the land. The contractors discovered a disused mineshaft, but believed it was filled with earth. Unknown to the defendant or the contractors, this mineshaft connected to the claimant's coalmine on neighbouring land. When the reservoir was filled, water poured down the shaft and flooded the mine. The defendant had not been negligent, as he had trusted the independent contractors, yet he was liable for the damage to the claimant's land. This case created a new area of tort.

Blackburn J defined the rule as:

> A person who, for his own purposes, brings onto land and keeps there anything likely to do mischief if it escapes, must do so at his peril, and, if he does not do so, he is *prima facie* answerable for all damage which is the natural consequence of its escape.

Lord Cairns added that the use of land has to be 'non-natural'.

Elements of the tort

The definition created by Blackburn J and Lord Cairns requires that the defendant bring something non-natural onto his/her land, for his/her own purposes, and that 'thing' must escape, causing damage of a foreseeable kind.

Brings onto land

The defendant must bring something onto his/her land for his/her own purposes that does not naturally occur there (*Giles* v *Walker*, 1890 and *Crowhurst* v *Amersham Burial Board*, 1878).

Non-natural use of land

Lord Cairns required the use of land to be 'non-natural'. What the courts define as 'non-natural' has been subject to change (*Rickards* v *Lothian*, 1913; *British Celanese* v *AH Hunt*, 1969; *Cambridge Water Co.* v *Eastern Counties Leather*, 1994; *Transco plc* v *Stockport Metropolitan Borough Council*, 2003).

Likely to do mischief

It must be foreseeable that the thing brought onto the land is likely to do mischief if it escapes. The escape itself does not have to be foreseeable.

Escape

The thing that is brought onto the land must escape from the defendant's land onto other land (*Read* v *Lyons*, 1946).

Damage

The escape must cause damage. The normal rules of causation apply in that damage must be reasonably foreseeable.

There can be no claim under *Rylands* v *Fletcher* for personal injury. This rule was first mentioned *obiter* by the House of Lords in the case of *Read* v *Lyons* (1947). It was confirmed in *Transco plc* v *Stockport Metropolitan Borough Council* (2003).

Who can sue and who can be sued

The rule in *Rylands* v *Fletcher* is a 'principle applicable between occupiers in respect of their land'. The claimant must therefore have some interest in the land that is affected (*Weller and Co.* v *Foot and Mouth Disease Research Institute*, 1996). The defendant must be the occupier who is in control of the land (*Smith* v *Scott*, 1973).

Defences
Act of a stranger

If the escape was caused by a stranger (a third party over whom the defendant had no control), this will be a defence. In *Rickards* v *Lothian* (1913), the tap that flooded the claimant's premises was turned on by a stranger, and the Privy Council decided that this was one of the reasons why the claim failed.

Volenti

It is a defence if the claimant consented to the defendant bringing the dangerous thing onto his/her land. This defence will be particularly strong if the thing on the defendant's land benefits the claimant. A common benefit (e.g. neighbours benefit from water storage on the defendant's land) will mean that a claim would fail if there was an escape.

Statutory authority

An Act of Parliament may authorise a dangerous activity, and therefore there can be no claim under *Rylands* v *Fletcher*. Some statutes specify if the rule applies and others do not, so it is up to the judge to decide (*Green* v *Chelsea Waterworks Co.*, 1894 and *Charing Cross Electricity Co.* v *Hydraulic Co.*, 1914).

Default of the claimant

If the escape and damage are caused completely by the default of the claimant, the defendant will not be liable. If the claimant is partly responsible, the normal rules of contributory negligence apply and the compensation will be reduced accordingly.

Act of God

Extreme weather conditions may afford a defence (*Nichols* v *Marsland*, 1876).

Evaluation

The rule in *Rylands* v *Fletcher* was a way of imposing liability in cases involving reservoirs and had the potential to extend to other dangerous activities during the Industrial Revolution. However, the rule was established so that it was difficult to prove, and it was restricted to occupiers of land. It could have gone much further and have become a way to deter landowners from allowing dangerous things on their land to escape, thus affording protection to the environment. Instead, the subsequent cases and the many defences mean that it applies in only a small number of situations.

The House of Lords in *Transco plc* v *Stockport Metropolitan Borough Council* (2003) discussed the future of *Rylands* v *Fletcher*. The two main criticisms of the rule are:
● it is difficult to prove owing to the many elements and the numerous defences
● it is strict liability

The House of Lords in *Transco plc* v *Stockport Metropolitan Borough Council* (2003) decided that the rule in *Rylands* v *Fletcher* should remain as it had been for 150 years, and there is still a small number of cases where the rule should be available. Lord Bingham suggested that there should be liability only where the defendant has done something where there is an 'exceptionally high risk of danger or mischief'. He also suggested that the term 'non-natural user' requires the defendant's use to be 'extraordinary and unusual'.

The Royal Commission on Civil Liability and Compensation for Personal Injury suggested that *Rylands* v *Fletcher* should be abolished, and that the government should have the power to impose strict liability on certain dangerous activities. The Law Commission suggested that the government could impose strict liability according to the concept of 'special danger', which would mean that the rule in *Rylands* v *Fletcher* would no longer be necessary. Some dangerous activities are already governed by Parliament. The **Consumer Protection Act 1987** governs defective products. It also imposes strict liability, as does the **Environmental Protection Act 1990** and other EU laws regarding health and safety

Liability for animals may arise under the common law or under the statutory rules contained in the **Animals Act 1971**.

A Common law

The common-law rules relating to liability for animals were replaced by the **Animals Act 1971**. It is possible, however, to bring a successful action in other torts, for example:

- negligence
- nuisance
- *Rylands* v *Fletcher*
- trespass to good, land and the person

Pitcher v *Martin* (1937)

The defendant's dog broke away from its lead, causing the claimant to fall. The defendant was liable in both nuisance and negligence.

Draper v *Hodder* (1972)

A pack of Jack Russell dogs savaged a child. There was no claim under the strict liability rules governing animals, as the dogs were not seen as dangerous. However, the claimant was successful in a claim in negligence, as the damage was foreseeable and the owner had breached his duty of care by failing to secure the dogs.

> A claim may be made in more than one tort.

B Animals Act 1971

As well as distinguishing between dangerous species (*ferae naturae*) and non-dangerous species (*mansuetae naturae*) of animal, the **Animals Act 1971** sets out the provisions for strict liability for damage done by animals:

> The provisions of sections 2 to 5 of this Act replace:
> (a) the rules of the common law imposing a strict liability in tort for damage done by an animal on the ground that the animal is regarded as *ferae naturae* [a wild animal] or that its vicious or mischievous propensities are known or presumed to be known;
> (b) subsections (1) and (2) of section 1 of the Dogs Act 1906 as amended by the Dogs (Amendment) Act 1928 (injury to cattle or poultry); and
> (c) the rules of the common law imposing a liability for cattle trespass.

The Act also provides liability for animals straying onto the highway.

The Act does not mention remoteness of damage, but owing to the strict liability nature of the law, it is assumed that it is limited to direct consequences rather than the Wagon Mound test of foreseeable damage. A keeper will not be liable under s.2(2) if he/she is not aware of the characteristic of the animals likely to lead to damage.

Dangerous species (ferae naturae)

A dangerous species is defined by s.6(2) of the **Animals Act 1971** as a species:
(a) not commonly domesticated in the British Isles; and
(b) whose fully grown animals normally have such characteristics that they are likely, unless restrained, to cause severe damage or that any damage that they may cause is likely to be severe

This definition of a dangerous species means that the only British animals that fit into this category are wild stags, foxes and wild cats.

An animal will be classed as dangerous even if it is domestic in its native country. For example, a camel is a domestic animal in certain parts of the world but would be classed as dangerous under the Act (*Tutin* v *Chipperfield Promotions Ltd*, 1980). In *Behrens* v *Bertram Mills Circus Ltd* (1957), an elephant was classed as a dangerous animal, even though it was described as 'no more dangerous than a cow'.

Section 6(2)(b) requires either that the dangerous animal is likely to cause severe damage (e.g. a tiger) or that any damage caused by the dangerous animal (even if this is unlikely to happen) is likely to be severe (e.g. an elephant may not be likely to cause damage, but if it does, it is likely to be severe because of the animal's size).

Under s.2(1), where any damage is caused by an animal which belongs to a dangerous species, any person who is a keeper of the animal is liable for the damage, except as otherwise provided by the Act.

The 'keeper' of the animal is responsible for it and is defined in s.6(3) as the person who:
(a) owns the animal or has it in his/her possession, or
(b) is the head of a household of which a member under the age of 16 owns the animal or has it in his/her possession

> A parent is responsible for the animals owned by his/her children.

Non-dangerous species (mansuetae naturae)

Liability for non-dangerous animals is defined in s.2(2) of the **Animals Act 1971**:

> Where damage is caused by an animal which does not belong to a dangerous species, a keeper of the animal is liable for the damage...if:
> (a) the damage is a kind which the animal, unless restrained, was likely to cause or which, if caused by the animal, was likely to be severe; and
> (b) the likelihood of the damage or of its being severe was due to characteristics of the animal which are not normally so found in animals of the same species or are not normally found except at particular times or in particular circumstances; and
> (c) those characteristics were known to that keeper or were at any time known to a person who at that time had charge of the animal as that keeper's servant or, where that keeper is the head of a household, were known to another keeper of the animal who is a member of that household and under the age of sixteen.

This lengthy definition requires the claimant to prove three things:
- Damage was likely to be caused or likely to be severe.

- The likelihood of the damage being caused or being severe was due to a characteristic of the animal in question (which is not usually common to that species or is only common at certain times).
- The characteristics were known to the 'keeper'.

Cummings v *Grainger* (1977)

The defendant kept an Alsatian guard dog on his scrap yard. The claimant was bitten by the dog when she entered the yard with a friend who was employee there.

Lord Denning took each part of s.2(2) in turn in order to establish liability:

(a) The animal in question was a dog of the Alsatian breed. If it did bite anyone, the damage was likely to be severe.
(b) The dog was a guard dog and 'it was due to those circumstances that the damage was likely to be severe if an intruder did enter on its territory'.
(c) 'Those characteristics were known to the keeper.'

The dog also displayed aggressive characteristics, which were not common to its breed. This was further evidence to satisfy s.2(2)(b).

All three parts of the test were satisfied, yet the defendant was not liable, as he had a defence (explained below).

Police dogs are trained to attack in certain circumstances, but this does not mean that they have abnormal characteristics. The ability to respond to instructions and training is a characteristic that is common in Alsatians. There was therefore no liability when an Alsatian police dog mistakenly bit a policeman while responding to instructions to chase a car thief (*Gloster* v *Chief Constable of Greater Manchester Police*, 2000).

2.1 Defences

Defences available for claims made under s.2 are contained in s.5 of the Act:

Highlight the key words in these three defences.

(1) A person is not liable under sections 2 to 4 of this Act for any damage which is due wholly to the fault of the person suffering it.
(2) A person is not liable under section 2 of the Act for any damage suffered by a person who voluntarily accepted the risk thereof.
(3) A person is not liable under section 2 of this Act for any damage caused by an animal kept on any premises or structure to a person trespassing there, if it is proved either:
  (a) that the animal was not kept there for the protection of persons or property; or
  (b) (if the animal was kept there for the protection of persons or property) that keeping it there for that purpose was not unreasonable.

Cummings v *Grainger* (1977)

Lord Denning did not think the claimant was wholly at fault for being bitten, so the defendant could not establish s.5(1). He did believe that s.5(3) was an available defence, as it was reasonable to keep a guard dog in a scrap yard in east London. Ormrod LJ thought that the defendant could also use s.5(2). He believed that the claimant accepted the risk, as she knew about the dog and admitted being frightened of it.

Since this case, the **Guard Dogs Act 1975** has made it a criminal offence to have a guard dog which is not under the control of a handler at all times. Contravention of this Act would mean that the use of a guard dog would be unreasonable for the purpose of s.5(3).

Contributory negligence may also be a defence under s.10 of the Act. The claimant's damages would be reduced accordingly.

3 *Trespassing livestock*

The law regarding trespassing livestock that cause damage is ancient. It was a strict liability law, which, in part, led to the rule in *Rylands* v *Fletcher* (1861). It is now governed by the **Animals Act 1971**.

Section 11 of the **Animals Act 1971** defines 'livestock' as cattle, horses, asses, mules, hinnies, sheep, pigs, goats, poultry, deer that are not wild and captive game birds.

> 'Livestock' does not include cats and dogs.

Liability for trespassing livestock is governed by s.4 of the **Animals Act 1971**:

(1) Where livestock belonging to any person strays onto land in the ownership or occupation of another and
  (a) damage is done by the livestock to the land or any property on it which is in the ownership or possession of the other person; or
  (b) any expenses are reasonably incurred by that other person in keeping the livestock…
  the person to whom the livestock belongs is liable for the damage or expenses, except as otherwise provided by this Act.

This is a strict liability tort, as it is not necessary for the keeper to be aware that there is a tendency for the livestock to stray.

Section 4(1)(a) states that the damage must be done to land or property. If there is personal injury, the claimant must instead claim for liability under s.2(2).

Section 4(1)(b) allows a claim for the expenses incurred in looking after the livestock while it is on the claimant's land.

Under s.7, the claimant may detain the animal until he/she receives compensation for the damage it has caused or the expenses incurred from looking after it. If the claimant does not receive payment within 14 days, he/she can sell the animal at public auction, keep the money owed and give the remainder to the animal's keeper. If the claimant is going to exercise this right of detention (formally known as 'distress damage feasant'), he/she must inform the police within 48 hours.

3.1 Defences

> Section 10 also allows the amount of damages awarded to be reduced according to contributory negligence on behalf of the claimant.

The defences to the liability for damage done by trespassing livestock are contained within s.5 of the **Animals Act 1971**.

Section 5(5) allows a defence where the livestock were on the highway in order to be moved. If the livestock stray onto other land while a person is driving them on the highway, there will be no liability unless there was negligence.

Matthews v *Wicks* (1987)

The defendant's sheep were grazing on common land and the highway. Some of the sheep trespassed in the claimant's garden and caused damage. The defendant could not rely on the defence contained in s.5(5), as it was not a lawful use of the highway.

Section 5(6) explains that there is no general duty in English law to fence animals. It will not be a defence for the defendant to say that the claimant should have fenced his/her land in order to prevent livestock entering it. If, however, there is a legal duty imposed on the claimant to fence his/her land and he/she does not, it will be a defence if livestock trespass.

4 Liability for injury to livestock caused by dogs

Section 9 of the **Animals Act 1971** makes it lawful to kill or injure a dog which:
(i) is worrying or is about to worry livestock, and there is no other reasonable means of ending or preventing the worrying, or
(ii) has been worrying livestock, has not left the vicinity, is not under the control of any person and there are no practicable means of ascertaining to whom it belongs

The person harming the dog must be entitled to protect the livestock (he/she must own the livestock or the land, or have been authorised by the owner) and is required to inform the police within 48 hours.

4.1 Defences

Under s.3 of the **Animals Act 1971**, the keeper of a dog that causes damage by killing or injuring livestock will be liable for damages, unless he/she can prove one of the following defences:
- fault of the claimant (s.5(1))
- assumption of risk (s.5(2))
- contributory negligence (s.10)
- livestock has strayed onto the land of the dog owner (s.5(4))

5 Animals straying onto the highway

Before the Animals Act was passed in 1971, there was no liability for damage caused to highway users when an animal strayed onto the highway. It was common for people to graze their animals on a village green and other common land such as the moors. This type of land is often unfenced. Since the passing of the Act, there is liability for such damage if a duty of care is owed, and it is governed by s.8. This law is therefore based on proving negligence.

Davies v *Davies* (1975)
The defendant grazed his sheep on common land where his mother was entitled to do so. The claimant collided with one of the defendant's sheep and claimed damages. The defendant was not liable under s.8, as he was licensed by the owner to graze his animals on the unfenced common land.

The **Registration of Commons Act 1971** required all people who were entitled to graze animals on common land to register.

Summary of Topic 6

Liability for animals may arise under the common law or under the statutory rules contained in the **Animals Act 1971**.

Common law

The common-law rules relating liability for animals have been replaced by the **Animals Act 1971**. It is possible, however, to bring a successful action in other torts, for example:

- negligence
- nuisance
- *Rylands* v *Fletcher*
- trespass to good, land and the person

In *Pitcher* v *Martin* (1937), the defendant's dog broke away from its lead, causing the claimant to fall. The defendant was liable in both nuisance and negligence.

Animals Act 1971

As well as distinguishing between dangerous species (*ferae naturae*) and non-dangerous species (*mansuetae naturae*), the **Animals Act 1971** sets out the provisions for strict liability for damage done by animals:

- trespassing livestock
- injury to livestock caused by dogs
- animals straying onto the highway

The Act does not mention remoteness of damage, but owing to the strict liability nature of the law, it is assumed that it is limited to direct consequences rather than the Wagon Mound test of foreseeable damage.

Dangerous species (*ferae naturae*)

A dangerous species is defined by s.6(2) of the **Animals Act 1971** as a species:

(a) not commonly domesticated in the British Isles; and

(b) whose fully grown animals normally have such characteristics that they are likely, unless restrained, to cause severe damage or that any damage that they may cause is likely to be severe

An animal will be classed as dangerous even if it is domestic in its native country (*Tutin* v *Chipperfield Promotions Ltd*, 1980 and *Behrens* v *Bertram Mills Circus Ltd*, 1957).

Section 6(2)(b) requires either that the dangerous animal is likely to cause severe damage (e.g. a tiger) or that any damage caused by the dangerous animal (even if this is unlikely to happen) is likely to be severe (e.g. an elephant may not be likely to cause damage, but if it does, it is likely to be severe because of the animal's size).

The 'keeper' of the animal is responsible for it and is defined in s.6(3) as the person who:

(a) owns the animal or has it in his/her possession, or

(b) is the head of a household of which a member under the age of 16 owns the animal or has it in his/her possession

Non-dangerous species (*mansuetae naturae*)

Liability for non-dangerous animals is defined in s.2(2) of the **Animals Act 1971**. The definition requires the claimant to prove three things:

- Damage was likely to be caused or likely to be severe.

- The likelihood of the damage being caused or being severe was due to a characteristic of the animal in question (which is not usually common to that species or is only common at certain times).
- The characteristics were known to the 'keeper' (*Cummings* v *Grainger*, 1977).

Police dogs are trained to attack in certain circumstances, but this does not mean that they have abnormal characteristics (*Gloster* v *Chief Constable of Greater Manchester Police*, 2000).

Defences

Defences available for claims made under s.2 are contained in s.5 of the Act:

(1) A person is not liable under sections 2 to 4 of this Act for any damage which is due wholly to the fault of the person suffering it.
(2) A person is not liable under section 2 of the Act for any damage suffered by a person who voluntarily accepted the risk thereof.
(3) A person is not liable under section 2 of this Act for any damage caused by an animal kept on any premises or structure to a person trespassing there, if it is proved either:
    (a) that the animal was not kept there for the protection of persons or property; or
    (b) (if the animal was kept there for the protection of persons or property) that keeping it there for that purpose was not unreasonable.

Contributory negligence may also be a defence under s.10 of the Act. The claimant's damages would be reduced accordingly.

Trespassing livestock

Section 11 of the **Animals Act 1971** defines 'livestock' as cattle, horses, asses, mules, hinnies, sheep, pigs, goats, poultry, deer that are not wild and captive game birds.

Liability for trespassing livestock is governed by s.4 of the **Animals Act 1971**:
- Section 4(1)(a) states that the damage must be done to land or property. If there is personal injury, the claimant must instead claim for liability under s.2(2).
- Section 4(1)(b) allows a claim for the expenses incurred in looking after the livestock while it is on the claimant's land.

Under s.7, the claimant may detain the animal until he/she receives compensation for the damage it has caused or the expenses incurred from looking after it. If the claimant does not receive payment within 14 days, he/she can sell the animal at public auction, keep the money owed and give the remainder to the animal's keeper. If the claimant is going to exercise this right of detention (formally known as 'distress damage feasant'), he/she must inform the police within 48 hours.

Defences

Section 5(5) allows a defence where the livestock were on the highway in order to be moved. If the livestock stray onto other land while a person is driving them on the highway, there will be no liability unless there was negligence (*Matthews* v *Wicks*, 1987).

Section 5(6) explains that there is no general duty in English law to fence animals. It will not be a defence for the defendant to say that the claimant should have fenced his/her land in order to prevent livestock entering it. If, however, there is a legal duty imposed on the claimant to fence his/her land and he/she does not, it will be a defence if livestock trespass.

Liability for injury to livestock caused by dogs

Section 9 of the **Animals Act 1971** makes it lawful to kill or injure a dog which:

(i) is worrying or is about to worry livestock, and there is no other reasonable means of ending or preventing the worrying, or

(ii) has been worrying livestock, has not left the vicinity, is not under the control of any person and there are no practicable means of ascertaining to whom it belongs

The person harming the dog must be entitled to protect the livestock (he/she must own the livestock or the land, or must have been authorised by the owner) and is required inform the police within 48 hours.

Defences

Under s.3 of the **Animals Act 1971**, the keeper of a dog that causes damage by killing or injuring livestock is liable for damages, unless he/she can prove one of the following defences:

- fault of the claimant (s.5(1))
- assumption of risk (s.5(2))
- contributory negligence (s.10)
- livestock has strayed onto the land of the dog owner (s.5(4))

Animals straying onto the highway

Before the Animals Act was passed in 1971, there was no liability for damage caused to highway users when an animal strayed onto the highway. Since the passing of the Act, there is liability for such damage if a duty of care is owed, and it is governed by s.8. This law is therefore based on proving negligence (*Davies* v *Davies*, 1975).

The tort of trespass to land is actionable per se, which means there is no need for any damage to have occurred. Trespass is committed when there is an intentional or negligent direct interference with land in the possession of the claimant.

A Land

The definition of land includes:
- the soil
- things attached to the soil, such as buildings and crops
- the ground beneath the soil
- the boundary
- the airspace above the soil

This does not mean that people who live beneath the flight path of an airport can claim for trespass to land, as the **Civil Aviation Act 1982** prevents such claims.

Bernstein v *Skyviews* (1978)
An aeroplane passing over the claimant's land taking photographs did not commit trespass. Griffith J said:

> I can find no support in authority for the view that a landowner's rights in the airspace above his property extend to an unlimited height. The problem is to balance the rights of an owner to enjoy the use of his land against the rights of the general public to take advantage of all that science now offers in the use of airspace. This balance in my judgement is to restrict the rights to such height as is necessary for the ordinary use and enjoyment of his land and the structures upon it; and declaring that above that height he has no greater rights in the air space than any other member of the public.

Under-soil rights may extend under a highway.

Cranes and advertising boards count as trespass (see *Woolerton and Wilson* v *Richard Costain Ltd*, 1970 and *Kelsen* v *Imperial Tobacco Co. Ltd*, 1956 on page 76).

Harrison v *Duke of Rutland* (1893)
Protesters standing along the highway adjacent to the claimant's land were trespassing when they shouted in order to scare the grouse that he was trying to shoot on his land.

Hickman v *Maisey* (1900)
The defendant was trespassing when he stood on the highway in order to spy on the claimant's racehorses while they trained on nearby land.

B Possession

While the claimant must be in possession of the land, he/she does not have to be the owner. The possessor has immediate and exclusive possession of the land. This means that for the purposes of this tort, a tenant would be classed as the possessor, rather than the landlord. Use of the land does not make someone a possessor entitled to claim for trespass, e.g. a guest, lodger or spectator cannot make a claim.

C Interference

The interference must be direct.

Esso Petroleum Co. v Southport Corporation (1956)
Oil spilled from the defendant's tanker into the waterways. The spill was not trespass, as it was thought to be indirect.

The interference must continue all the time that it is on the land.

Holmes v Wilson (1839)
Buttresses were placed on the claimant's land to support a road that was being built. This amounted to trespass. The Highways Authority failed to remove the buttresses and the claimant successfully claimed for trespass again.

Direct interference can be committed in many ways.

Woolerton and Wilson v Richard Costain Ltd (1970)
A crane swinging over the claimant's land will amount to trespass.

Kelsen v Imperial Tobacco Co. Ltd (1956)
It will be considered trespass if an advertising hoarding overhangs the claimant's land.

A lawful visitor may become a trespasser by:
- going beyond his/her permission (e.g. a guest in a hotel would become a trespasser if he/she entered the kitchens), or
- staying on the land longer than he/she should (e.g. a spectator who stays on a sports ground after a match has finished)

If the defendant has a lawful right to be on the land (granted by common law or statute) but then becomes a trespasser by committing a wrongful act, this is known as trespass *ab initio*.

Six Carpenters (1610)
The defendants went into an inn where they bought food and drink. They ordered more things but refused to pay. Their lawful right to be in the inn was followed by a wrongful act, which made them trespassers. However, the men were not liable because the wrongful act was in fact an omission (refusing to pay), which will not constitute a direct interference.

This rule has been criticised, as it is held that the law should not act retrospectively (*Chic Fashion (West Wales) Ltd* v *Jones*, 1968). A lawful entry should not become unlawful at a later time. However, the rule was applied in the later case of *Cinnamond* v *British Airports Authority* (1980), when minicab divers were unlawfully touting for business.

Throwing something onto the land or allowing animals onto the land will amount to trespass.

League Against Cruel Sports Ltd v Scott (1986)
The claimants owned parts of Dartmoor, where they did not allow hunting of the wild deer. The master of a hunt was liable for trespass when some of his hounds wandered onto the claimants' land.

D Intention or negligence

The trespass must be voluntary.

Smith v Stone (1647)

The defendant was not trespassing when he was thrown onto the claimant's land by force.

The claimant must prove that the defendant negligently or intentionally entered the land.

For the facts of this case, see page 76.

League Against Cruel Sports Ltd v Scott (1986)

This case established that entry onto the land can be committed negligently: 'The master will be liable for trespass if he intended to cause the hounds to enter such land or if by his failure to exercise proper control over them he causes them to enter such land.'

It does not matter whether or not the defendant negligently or intentionally trespasses, as long as his/her entry is intentional or negligent.

Basely v Clarkson (1682)

The defendant trespassed on the claimant's land when he cut the grass and moved it, mistakenly thinking that it was his.

E Defences

1 Volenti

The claimant gave his/her permission (consent) for the defendant to enter the land.

2 *Lawful justification*

A person may have a right to enter the claimant's land. This right may be conferred by:
- statute, e.g. the **Police and Criminal Evidence Act 1984** allows the police entry onto land, and the **Rights of Entry (Gas and Electricity Boards) Act 1954** allows meter readings to be taken
- common law, e.g. to abate a nuisance
- prescription

Prescription is where someone gains a right to do something because of long use.

3 *Necessity*

This defence allows the defendant to trespass if there is an emergency, such as to help someone or to put out a fire.

The defence of necessity was used successfully in *Saltpetre Case* (1606), when the defendant trespassed on the claimant's land to defend the realm. The use of this defence today is allowed only when there is no reasonable alternative available to the defendant.

***Rigby* v *Chief Constable of Northamptonshire* (1985)**
The police were not trespassing when they threw CS gas into a shop in order to catch a dangerous criminal who had gone in. However, they *were* negligent when they did not call the fire brigade when the shop caught fire.

4 Licences

The person in possession of the land can grant licences to people to allow either express or implied permission to be on the land. A person would become a trespasser if he/she were to exceed the permission given in the licence.

5 Jus tertii

It will be a defence in trespass if the defendant can prove that the land belongs to a third person, rather than to the claimant.

Summary of Topic 7

The tort of trespass to land is actionable per se, which means there is no need for any damage to have occurred. Trespass is committed when there is an intentional or negligent direct interference with land in the possession of the claimant.

Land

The definition of land includes:
- the soil
- things attached to the soil, such as buildings and crops
- the ground underneath the soil
- the boundary
- the airspace above the soil that is necessary for the enjoyment of land (e.g. *Bernstein* v *Skyviews*, 1978).

Cranes and advertising boards count as trespass (*Woolerton and Wilson* v *Richard Costain Ltd*, 1970 and *Kelsen* v *Imperial Tobacco Co. Ltd*, 1956).

Under-soil rights may extend under a highway (*Harrison* v *Duke of Rutland*, 1893 and *Hickman* v *Maisey*, 1900).

Possession

While the claimant must be in possession of the land, he/she does not have to be the owner. The possessor has immediate and exclusive possession of the land. This means that for the purposes of this tort, a tenant would be classed as the possessor, rather than the landlord.

Interference

The interference must be direct (*Esso Petroleum Co.* v *Southport Corporation*, 1956) and continue all the time that it is on the land (*Holmes* v *Wilson*, 1839).

Things which overhang the land may be trespass (*Woolerton and Wilson* v *Richard Costain Ltd*, 1970 and *Kelsen* v *Imperial Tobacco Co. Ltd*, 1956).

A lawful visitor may become a trespasser by:
- going beyond his/her permission, or
- staying on the land longer than he/she should

If the defendant has a lawful right to be on the land (granted by common law or statute) but then becomes a trespasser by committing a wrongful act, this is known as trespass *ab initio* (*Six Carpenters*, 1610).

Throwing something onto the land or allowing animals onto the land will amount to trespass (*League Against Cruel Sports Ltd* v *Scott*, 1986).

Intention or negligence

The trespass must be voluntary (*Smith* v *Stone*, 1647).

The claimant must prove that the defendant negligently or intentionally entered the land (*League Against Cruel Sports Ltd* v *Scott*, 1986).

It does not matter whether or not the defendant negligently or intentionally trespasses, as long as his/her entry is intentional or negligent (*Basely* v *Clarkson*, 1682).

Defences

Volenti

The claimant gave his/her permission (consent) for the defendant to enter the land.

Lawful justification

A person may have a right to enter the claimant's land. This right may be conferred by:
- statute, e.g. the **Police and Criminal Evidence Act 1984** allows the police entry onto land, and the **Rights of Entry (Gas and Electricity Boards) Act 1954** allows meter readings to be taken
- common law, e.g. to abate a nuisance
- prescription

Necessity

This defence allows the defendant to trespass if there is an emergency, such as to help someone or to put out a fire (*Rigby* v *Chief Constable of Northamptonshire*, 1985).

Licences

The person in possession of the land can grant licences to people to allow either express or implied permission to be on the land. A person would become a trespasser if he/she were to exceed the permission given in the licence.

Jus tertii

It will be a defence in trespass if the defendant can prove that the land belongs to a third person, rather than to the claimant.

Trespass to the person involves a direct interference with a person's rights over his/her body or personal security. As with other types of trespass, trespass to the person is actionable per se, so the claimant need not prove any damage or injury, merely that the tort has been committed. It is one of the oldest torts and can be committed in three different ways:

- by assault
- by battery
- by false imprisonment

A Assault

The definition of assault was defined in the case of *Collins* v *Wilcock* (1984) as 'an act which causes another person to apprehend the infliction of immediate, unlawful force on his person'.

1 Elements

An assault is any act which makes the victim fear that unlawful force is about to be used against him/her. No force need actually be applied, and actions such as raising a fist, pointing a gun or brandishing a sword will be sufficient. The key question is the effect that the defendant's actions have on the claimant. If the claimant perceives the threat of violence, it does not matter that no force is actually applied.

There must be activity by the defendant — a passive state will not usually constitute an assault.

Innes v *Wylie* (1844)
There was no assault when a police officer stood and blocked a doorway, preventing the claimant from passing.

If the defendant attempts to inflict force but is prevented from doing so, this will still amount to an assault.

Stephens v *Myers* (1830)
The defendant committed an assault by waving a clenched fist at the claimant, despite the fact that he was restrained by a third party and unable to reach the claimant.

The victim must fear *immediate* threat of harm, not at some time in the future.

The courts have sometimes given a fairly generous interpretation of the concept of immediacy.

Thomas v *NUM (South Wales Area)* (1985)
There was no assault when striking miners made violent gestures at a miner who broke the picket line during a strike. The claimant was on a bus and the miners gesturing on the picket line were behind police barricades. It was held that there was no threat of immediate violence.

Smith v *Chief Superintendent, Woking Police Station* (1983)
The victim was at home in her ground-floor flat dressed in her nightdress. She was terrified when she suddenly saw the defendant standing in her garden staring at her through the window. The court held he was liable for assault, on the grounds

that the victim feared immediate infliction of force, even though she was safely locked inside the building.

For many years, the courts have debated whether words can amount to an assault.

R v *Meade and Belt* (1823)

People were gathered around a house and started to sing menacing songs and to use violent language. Judge Holroyd said that 'no words or singing are equivalent to an assault'. However in *R* v *Wilson* (1955), Lord Goddard stated of the accused: 'He called out "Get out the knives", which itself would be an assault.' As *Wilson* is a more recent case, this outcome is preferred.

More recently, the House of Lords decided that a silent telephone call can constitute an assault (*R* v *Constanza*, 1997 and *R* v *Ireland and Burstow*, 1997). It is thought that this will now also be the position in civil law, although there has not, as yet, been a case to confirm this principle.

There is no assault if it is obvious to the victim that the defendant cannot or will not carry out his/her threat of violence.

Tuberville v *Savage* (1669)

Annoyed by someone's comments to him, the defendant put his hand on his sword, which by itself would have been enough to constitute an assault. However, at the same time he said: 'If it were not assize time I would not take such language.' This meant that since judges were hearing criminal cases in town at the time, he had no intention of using violence. His accompanying words prevented his actions from amounting to assault, since they clearly indicated that there was no danger of immediate force being inficted upon the claimant.

Words can negate or cancel out what would otherwise be an assault.

In terms of the defendant's state of mind, he/she must have intended the claimant to apprehend the infliction of immediate force. In other words, he/she must have intended to frighten the claimant (enough to amount to an assault) but does not need to have intended actually to inflict force on the claimant.

B Battery

Battery is the application of unlawful force on another. It often follows on from assault but it need not do. There can be an assault without battery, for example when force is threatened but never actually used. There can also be battery without an assault, for example if the defendant strikes the claimant on the head from behind. Any unlawful physical contact can amount to a battery. There is no need to prove harm or pain — a mere touch can be sufficient.

Battery is defined in *Cole* v *Turner* (1704) as 'the least touching of another in anger'.

1 *Elements*

It is settled law that there can be a battery where there has been no direct contact with the victim's body—touching his/her clothing may be enough to constitute this offence, even if the victim feels nothing as a result. There need not be violence or injury.

Nash v *Sheen* (1953)

The defendant hairdresser who caused a rash by mistakenly applying a tone rinse to the claimant's hair was liable for battery.

It has long been accepted that some forms of physical contact are not actionable, as stated by Goff LJ in *Collins* v *Wilcock* (1984):

> Nobody can complain of the jostling which is inevitable from his presence in, for example, a supermarket, an underground station or a busy street; nor can a person who attends a party complain if his hand is seized in friendship, or even if his back is (within reason) slapped…Among such forms of conduct, long held to be acceptable, is touching a person for the purpose of engaging his attention, though of course using no more greater degree of physical contact than is reasonably necessary in the circumstances for that purpose.

Some argue that this is because in such instances there is no hostility, while others claim that there is implied consent to such contact.

The touch must be hostile, although there is no definitive guide as to what this amounts to — it is simply a question of fact to be decided in each case.

Wilson v *Pringle* (1986)

The claimant schoolboy was injured when falling, after the defendant pulled his shoulder bag during horseplay. The Court of Appeal stated that the touching must be proved to be hostile, although it did not define what this meant.

In terms of the defendant's mental state, he/she must intend to apply physical force to the claimant. A careless touch will not be sufficient.

Letang v *Cooper* (1965)

The claimant was injured while sunbathing outside a hotel, when the defendant negligently, but not deliberately, drove over her legs. There was no battery since the defendant did not intend to apply physical force to the claimant's legs.

Assault and battery are also criminal offences and are perhaps more usually dealt with in the criminal rather than the civil sphere, with victims seeking compensation from the Criminal Injuries Compensation Scheme rather than through the civil courts.

C False imprisonment

False in this sense means 'wrongful'.

Imprisonment generally refers to the restriction of a person's liberty or freedom of movement. The tort of false imprisonment arises when such deprivation is enforced without lawful excuse, often in the context of arrest by the police or security guards.

1 *Elements*

It is possible to commit this tort without physical imprisonment, since it merely requires that the person's liberty be restrained.

A person need not be locked up — for example in a cell — as long as there is a total restraint on his/her liberty. This may be physical and take the form of holding onto someone so that he/she cannot escape, or it may be non-physical, for example intimidating words or threats.

False imprisonment

There must be a total restraint on the person's freedom of movement in every direction.

Bird v Jones (1845)

The defendant set up a seating area on Hammersmith Bridge and charged those who wanted to watch a boat race. The claimant attempted to walk through the area but refused to pay. The defendant would not let him pass and the claimant sued for false imprisonment. As the claimant could have crossed to the other side of the bridge, the defendant was not liable. The restraint on the claimant's liberty was not total.

If there is a reasonable escape route, there is no false imprisonment. However, if the claimant had a means of escape but was unaware of it, he/she may still claim for false imprisonment unless the reasonable person would have realised that escape in this way was possible. An example might be if the defendant locked the claimant in a room in which, unbeknown to the claimant, there was a spare key.

Robinson v Balmain Ferry Company (1910)

Notices at the defendant ferry company's wharf stated that it cost a penny to enter or leave it. The claimant paid a penny to enter so that he could take a ferry crossing. Once through the turnstile, he changed his mind and asked to be let out. The defendant prevented him leaving until he had paid another penny. The court held that this was not false imprisonment as he had voluntarily put himself into the situation and the conditions imposed by the ferry company were not unreasonable. Additionally, the claimant could have left by taking the ferry.

> It is not false imprisonment just because the claimant has to pay to leave.

Herd v Weardale Steel, Coal and Coke Co. (1915)

The claimant was a miner who had a dispute with his manager during a shift. He refused to complete a task that he considered dangerous and demanded to be returned to the surface. The defendant company would not take him until the end of his shift. The court held that this was not false imprisonment; indeed, the miner was in breach of his contract and did not have the right to demand to be taken to the surface 5 hours before the end of his shift. Had the company detained him after his shift had finished, then it would have been false imprisonment.

> An additional reason for the finding in this case is that false imprisonment must be brought about by an act and not an omission. Here, the company simply failed to allow the claimant to leave the mineshaft.

The question has arisen as to whether the claimant must be aware that he or she is being detained.

Meering v Grahame-White Aviation Co. (1920)

The claimant was employed by the defendants and was asked to go to their office to be questioned about a theft. The claimant was unaware that two policemen were waiting outside the office door in order to prevent him from leaving. When the claimant became aware of this, he sued for false imprisonment. The Court of Appeal said that the defendants were liable, despite the fact that the claimant did not know that he was being detained.

Lord Atkins stated:

> It appears to me that a person could be imprisoned without his knowing it. I think a person can be imprisoned while he is asleep, while he is in a state of drunkenness, while he is unconscious, and while he is a lunatic…It is quite unnecessary to go on to show that in fact the man knew that he was imprisoned.

The amount of damages awarded is usually less if the claimant was unaware of his/her detention at the time of its occurrence.

This tort could therefore be committed while someone was unconscious or asleep.

Murray v *Ministry of Defence* (1988) confirmed *obiter* that it is not necessary for a person unlawfully detained to prove that he/she knew that he/she was being detained. It was not directly relevant in this case, as the claimant was aware that she was being detained.

There is no minimum period for which a person must be detained before he/she has a claim for false imprisonment. However, the amount of time of being detained and the degree of harm suffered will be taken into account when assessing the level of damages to be awarded.

The defendant's mental state is not relevant, since false imprisonment is a tort of strict liability.

R v *Governor of Brockhill Prison ex parte Evans (No. 2)* (2000)

The House of Lords held that the governor of a prison was liable for false imprisonment when a claimant's prison sentence was incorrectly calculated and she was kept imprisoned for too long a period. This was despite the fact that the governor was not personally at fault.

D Defences to trespass to the person

1 Consent

Consent can operate as a full defence to assault, battery or false imprisonment. The usual rules regarding consent apply (see Topic 9).

1.1 Sports

In terms of trespass to the person, the issue of consent frequently arises in relation to sporting activities where a participant is injured by another while taking part. The general rule is that by agreeing to play, competitors consent to the usual risks of that sport. Thus, if a claimant is playing football, he/she cannot usually complain about any injury sustained in the usual course of a match. If the injury was inflicted outside of the rules, however, then consent will probably not be available as a defence.

1.2 Medical treatment

The issue of consent also arises in relation to medical treatment. Without consent, a claimant would have a claim for trespass to the person. There are many issues surrounding consent, for example if the claimant received treatment that he/she had not consented to at all.

Potts v *North West RHA* (1983)

The claimant received damages after being given an injection of a contraceptive drug without her prior knowledge or consent.

A patient may refuse to consent to an operation. The general rule is that a patient does have the right to refuse medical treatment as long as he/she is fully competent.

B v *An NHS Trust* (2002)

The claimant was paralysed from the neck down and was placed on a ventilator to assist with her breathing. Following an operation, she was able to speak and requested that the ventilator be turned off. The court allowed this even though it would result in her death. Without her consent, keeping her on a ventilator amounted to trespass.

However, the courts sometimes overrule a seemingly competent patient's refusal to consent.

Re T (1992)

The claimant was pregnant. After spending time with her mother, who was a Jehovah's Witness, she signed a form refusing to consent to a blood transfusion. The Court of Appeal held that she had not been properly advised of the consequences of her refusal and considered that her mother may have unduly influenced her. As such, it overruled her wishes and allowed the operation.

1.3 Valid consent

The consent of the claimant will be valid only if he/she understands the nature of the act and knows exactly what he/she is consenting to. The victim must have the capacity to consent — children and those suffering from mental illness may not therefore be able to give valid consent.

Following *Gillick* v *West Norfolk and Wisbech AHA* (1986), parents may give consent on behalf of their child until the child has sufficient understanding of what is proposed. This is sometimes termed 'Gillick competence'.

Gillick v *West Norfolk and Wisbech AHA* (1986)

Guidance was issued by the Department of Health and Social Security to area health authorities, which contained a section dealing with contraceptive advice and treatment for young people. It stated that in exceptional cases, a doctor could decide to prescribe contraception to someone under 16.

The claimant, who was the mother of five girls under 16, wrote to her local area health authority seeking an assurance from them that no contraceptive advice or treatment would be given to any of her daughters while under 16 without her knowledge and consent. The area health authority refused to give such an assurance and the claimant challenged the guidance. The House of Lords said that children under 16 could give valid consent to contraceptive advice and treatment as long as they had sufficient maturity and intelligence to understand the nature and implications of such treatment. This was for the doctor to decide.

2 Self-defence

A defendant may be able to rely on self-defence to escape liability if he/she has used force to protect himself/herself, another person or property. The defence will be available only if the force used is deemed to have been 'reasonable'. What is 'reasonable' depends on the facts of each case, but there is usually a consideration of proportionality in terms of the seriousness of the threat compared with the amount of force used. Put simply, if the amount of force used by the defendant matches the level of threat faced, then the defence will usually succeed; however, if the defendant uses excessive force, the defence will usually fail.

Lane v *Holloway* (1967)

The defendant punched the drunken claimant after he had called the defendant's wife a 'monkey-faced tart'. The injury to the claimant's eye required 19 stitches. The court held that the force was not in proportion to the threat from the claimant and the defendant was not able to rely on self-defence.

Revill v *Newbury* (1996)

Self-defence did not apply when the claimant burglar was injured after the 76-year-old defendant, disturbed while sleeping in his shed, fired a shotgun through a hole in the shed door. It was thought that the force was excessive.

Lawful authority and detention

A person may be lawfully arrested and, if so, has no claim for false imprisonment. Matters of arrest generally involve the police, and they may well question an individual prior to any arrest. While the police may question individuals, those individuals are entirely free to decline to answer unless arrested. This was confirmed in the case of *Rice* v *Connolly* (1966). However, there is a thin line between lawfully refusing to answer questions and obstructing the police (*Ricketts* v *Cox*, 1982).

The main statute governing police powers is the **Police and Criminal Evidence Act 1984** (PACE), although there are various others. These include the **Misuse of Drugs Act 1971**, the **Criminal Justice and Public Order Act 1994** and the **Terrorism Act 2000**. To supplement PACE, the Home Office has issued codes of practice that detail the provisions.

Under s.1 of PACE, the police have the power to stop and search individuals. A search occurs when the police stop an individual and search him/her, his/her clothes or anything that he/she is carrying. Code A states that powers to stop and search must be used fairly, with respect and without discrimination. An individual can be stopped and searched only if the police have reasonable suspicion that the suspect has on his/her person drugs, weapons or stolen property, or things that could be used to commit a crime, an act of terrorism or criminal damage. The suspicion should be based on facts, intelligence, information or behaviour. It cannot be based on personal factors, including age, race, religion, appearance, previous convictions or generalisations, stereotypes or any of these factors in combination.

An individual must be informed that he/she is being stopped so that a search may be carried out. He/she must be informed of the officer's name or number and the station to which the officer is attached, given an explanation of the grounds upon which the search is being carried out and informed of the object of the search. If the officer is not in uniform, he/she must provide identification (PACE s.2(3)).

Defences to trespass to the person

An individual can be stopped and searched in a public place or anywhere else if the police believe that the person has committed a crime. If the search is in a public place, the suspect can be required to remove only his/her coat or jacket and gloves. If the police wish the suspect to remove anything else, they must take him/her to a nearby place out of public view. If the individual protests, reasonable force may be used (PACE s.117). If the police recover any stolen or prohibited articles, these can be seized (PACE s.1(6)).

Section 3 of the **Criminal Justice Act 1967** allows the use of reasonable force in order to prevent a crime, or to lawfully arrest or detain a person unlawfully at large.

> As long as the force is reasonable, there can be no claim for assault or battery.

3.1 Powers of arrest

The powers of arrest under PACE have recently been amended by the **Serious Organised Crime and Police Act 2005** and a new code. Code G has been issued, giving guidance on the exercise of the powers of arrest. The police are permitted to arrest:

- anyone who is about to commit an offence or who is committing an offence
- anyone the officer has reasonable grounds for suspecting is about to commit an offence
- anyone who is reasonably suspected of being guilty of an offence that the officer has reasonable grounds for suspecting has been committed
- anyone guilty of an offence that has been committed

The powers of arrest, which apply to any offence, are subject to the necessity test — the officer must believe that it is necessary to arrest that person. Reasons why an arrest might be necessary are set out in s.2 of Code G and include the need to:

- ascertain the name of the person involved or his/her address
- prevent the person causing injury to himself/herself or others
- prevent the person causing damage to property

Code G confirms that the right to liberty is a fundamental human right, and since the powers of arrest interfere with that right, officers must be fully justified in using them. It states that two tests must be met before an arrest can be said to be lawful:

(a) The person must be involved or suspected of involvement or attempted involvement in a crime.

(b) There must be reasonable grounds for believing that the person's arrest is necessary.

The person must be informed by the arresting officers of the fact of his/her arrest and the reason for it — even if this is obvious. He/she must then be cautioned.

3.2 Detention

3.2a Arrival at the station

Once arrested, the suspect must be taken to the police station as soon as possible. On arrival at the station, he/she will be taken to the custody officer, who will assess the strength of the evidence against the person. On the basis of this, the custody officer will decide whether the suspect can be charged. If so, the suspect will be charged and usually released on bail.

If there is not enough evidence to charge the suspect at that stage, he/she will be detained so that the police have time to gather the necessary evidence. Often, police will try to obtain the required evidence by interviewing the suspect. The suspect has a right to have someone informed of his/her detention and told where he/she is being held. This can be delayed if the detention relates to an indictable offence and the delay is considered necessary to protect evidence or prevent harm to others.

3.2b Time limits

The police are not allowed to detain a suspect indefinitely, and the custody officer is required to review the need for detention regularly. The custody officer will review whether there is enough evidence to charge after the first 6 hours. Further reviews are carried out every 9 hours. Generally, the police can detain suspects for up to 36 hours, timed from their arrival at the station. This may be extended for a further 12 hours by the police, but it must be done by an officer of superintendent rank or above. A further and final extension of up to 96 hours is permitted, but this must be approved by a magistrate.

3.2c Search at the station

A suspect may be searched, or have samples taken, while at the police station. An example would be a breath or blood sample if drink driving were suspected. Again, the procedures are laid out in the relevant statutes, including PACE, and the person would have no claim for trespass against the person if such procedures were followed correctly.

E Harassment

This area is governed by the **Protection from Harassment Act 1997**, as amended by the **Serious Organised Crime and Police Act 2005**. Both are recent statutes that were passed in response to a number of high-profile stalking cases.

The legislation prohibits harassment. Section 1 of the **Protection from Harassment Act 1997**, as amended, states that:

> A person must not pursue a course of conduct…which amounts to harassment of another, and…which he knows or ought to know amounts to harassment of the other.

By virtue of the **Serious Organised Crime and Police Act 2005**, the same provision applies to the harassment of two or more people intended to persuade the victims either not to do something that they are entitled or required to do, or instead to do something that they are not under any obligation to do.

Harassment itself is not defined but includes alarming the person or causing them distress. The Act states that 'conduct' includes speech.

Section 2 of the **Protection from Harassment Act 1997** states that the person whose course of conduct is in question ought to know that it amounts to or involves harassment of another, if a reasonable person in possession of the same information would think that it amounted to harassment. Thus, a defendant would not be able to argue that he/she did not intend to cause the victim harassment if a reasonable person, on the same facts, would realise that it would be the probable result.

The statutes prohibit a 'course of conduct'. When an individual is being harassed, this must involve conduct on at least two occasions. If two or more people are being harassed, a course of conduct means conduct directed at each person on at least one occasion. However, what amounts to a 'course of conduct' is generally a matter to be decided by the courts.

Pratt v *DPP* (2001)

The defendant was charged with harassing his wife. The question was whether his actions amounted to a course of conduct. In the first incident, the defendant had tried to start an argument with his wife, followed her into the kitchen and threw a beaker of water over her. On the second occasion, the defendant chased his wife through the house and up the stairs, swearing and repeatedly questioning her.

It was held that the two incidents did amount to a course of conduct. They had taken place within 3 months of each other and were inextricably connected.

A person who pursues such a course of conduct is guilty of a criminal offence, but the legislation also provides a civil remedy. The claimant may be awarded damages for any anxiety or financial loss caused by the harassment. Additionally, victims may apply for an injunction to restrain the person harassing them. Having a civil as well as a criminal remedy means that there are two an alternative means of protection available to the victim. If the criminal sanction is inappropriate or the standard of proof cannot be met, the civil option is available. It also allows the defendant to be restrained by an injunction if the evidence shows that an offence is likely to be committed.

Summary of Topic 8

Trespass to the person involves a direct interference with a person's rights over his/her body or personal security. It is actionable per se, so the claimant need not prove any damage or injury, merely that the tort has been committed.

Assault

Elements

An assault is any act which makes the victim fear that unlawful force is about to be used against him/her. No force need actually be applied; the key question is the effect that the defendant's actions have on the claimant. If the claimant perceives the threat of violence, it does not matter that no force is actually applied. There must be activity by the defendant — a passive state will not usually constitute an assault (*Innes* v *Wylie*, 1844).

If the defendant attempts to inflict force but is prevented from doing so, this will still amount to an assault (*Stephens* v *Myers*, 1830).

The victim must fear *immediate* threat of harm, not at some time in the future (*Thomas* v *NUM (South Wales Area)*,1985).

There is no assault if it is obvious to the victim that the defendant cannot or will not carry out his threat of violence.

For many years, the courts have debated whether words can amount to an assault. Recently, the House of Lords decided that words or even a silent telephone call can constitute an assault (*R* v *Constanza*, 1997 and *R* v *Ireland and Burstow*, 1997). It is thought that this will now also be the position in civil law, although there has not yet been a case to confirm this principle. Words can also negate or cancel out what would otherwise be an assault (*Tuberville* v *Savage*, 1669).

In terms of the defendant's state of mind, he/she must have intended the claimant to apprehend the infliction of immediate force. In other words, he/she must have intended to frighten the claimant (enough to amount to an assault) but does not need to have intended actually to inflict force on the claimant.

Battery

Battery is the application of unlawful force on another. It often follows on from assault but it need not do. Any unlawful physical contact can amount to a battery; there is no need to prove harm or pain, and a mere touch can be sufficient.

Elements

It is settled law that there can be a battery where there has been no direct contact with the victim's body — touching his/her clothing may be enough to constitute this offence, even if the victim feels nothing as a result. There is no need for violence or injury (*Nash* v *Sheen*, 1953).

Some forms of physical contact are not actionable, such as jostling or handshaking.

The touch must be hostile, although there is no definitive guide as to what this amounts to — it is simply a question of fact to be decided in each case.

Defendant's state of mind

In terms of the defendant's mental state, he/she must intend to apply physical force to the claimant. A careless touch will not be sufficient (*Letang* v *Cooper*, 1965).

Assault and battery are also criminal offences and are perhaps more usually dealt with in the criminal rather than the civil sphere, with victims seeking compensation from the Criminal Injuries Compensation Scheme rather than through the civil courts.

False imprisonment

Imprisonment generally refers to the restriction of a person's liberty or freedom of movement. The tort of false imprisonment arises when such deprivation is enforced without lawful excuse, often in the context of arrest by the police or security guards.

Elements

A person need not be locked up — for example in a cell — as long as there is a total restraint on his/her liberty. This may be physical and take the form of holding onto someone so that he/she cannot escape, or it may be non-physical, for example intimidating words or threats. There must be a total restraint on the person's freedom of movement in every direction (*Bird* v *Jones*, 1845).

If there is a reasonable escape route, there is no false imprisonment. However, if the claimant had a means of escape but was unaware of it, he/she may still claim for false imprisonment unless the reasonable person would have realised that escape in this way was possible.

It is not necessary for a person unlawfully detained to prove that he/she knew that he/she was being detained (*Meering* v *Grahame-White Aviation Co.*, 1920 and *Murray* v *Ministry of Defence*, 1988).

There is no minimum period for which a person must be detained before he/she has a claim for false imprisonment. However, the amount of time of being detained and the degree of harm suffered will be taken into account when assessing the level of damages to be awarded.

Defendant's state of mind

The defendant's mental state is not relevant, since false imprisonment is a tort of strict liability.

Defences to trespass to the person

Consent

Consent can operate as a full defence to assault, battery or false imprisonment.

Sports

In terms of trespass to the person, the issue of consent frequently arises in relation to sporting activities where a participant is injured by another while taking part. The general rule is that by agreeing to play, competitors consent to the usual risks of that sport. If the injury was inflicted outside of the rules, however, then consent will probably not be available as a defence.

Medical treatment

The issue of consent also arises in relation to medical treatment. Without consent, a claimant would have a claim for trespass to the person. A patient may refuse to consent to an operation. The general rule is that a patient does have the right to refuse medical treatment as long as he/she is fully competent (*B* v *An NHS Trust*, 2002). However, the courts sometimes overrule a seemingly competent patient's refusal to consent (*Re T*, 1992).

Valid consent

The consent of the claimant will be valid only if he/she understands the nature of the act and knows exactly what he/she is consenting to. The victim must have the capacity to consent — children and those suffering from mental illness may not therefore be able to give valid consent. Following *Gillick* v *West Norfolk and Wisbech AHA* (1986), parents may give consent on behalf of their child until the child has sufficient understanding of what is proposed. This is sometime termed 'Gillick competence'.

Self-defence

A defendant may be able to rely on self-defence to escape liability if he/she has used force to protect himself/herself, another person or property. The defence will be available only if the force used is deemed to have been 'reasonable'. What is 'reasonable' depends on the facts of each case, but there is usually a consideration of proportionality in terms of the seriousness of the threat compared to the amount of force used. If the defendant uses excessive force, the defence will usually fail (*Lane* v *Holloway*, 1967 and *Revill* v *Newbury*, 1996).

Lawful authority and detention

A person may be lawfully arrested and, if so, has no claim for false imprisonment. An arrest will usually involve the police; the main statute governing police powers is the **Police and Criminal Evidence Act 1984** (PACE), although there are various others, including the **Misuse of Drugs Act 1971**, the **Criminal Justice and Public Order Act 1994** and the **Terrorism Act 2000**.

Under s.1 of PACE, the police have the power to stop and search individuals. An individual can be stopped and searched only if the police have reasonable suspicion that the suspect has on his/her person drugs, weapons or stolen property, or things that could be used to commit a crime, an act of terrorism or criminal damage. If the individual protests, the police may use reasonable force (PACE s.117). If the police recover any stolen or prohibited articles, these can be seized under PACE s.1 (6).

Section 3 of the **Criminal Justice Act 1967** allows the use of reasonable force in order to prevent a crime, or to lawfully arrest or detain a person unlawfully at large. As long as the force is reasonable, there can be no claim for assault or battery.

Powers of arrest

The powers of arrest under PACE have been amended by the **Serious Organised Crime and Police Act 2005**. Two tests must now be met before an arrest can be said to be lawful:

- The person must be involved or suspected of involvement or attempted involvement in a crime.
- There must be reasonable grounds for believing that the person's arrest is necessary.

Detention

Arrival at the station

Once arrested, the suspect must be taken to the police station as soon as possible. On arrival at the station, he/she will be taken to the custody officer, who will assess the strength of the evidence against the person. On the basis of this, the custody officer will decide whether the suspect can be charged. If so, the suspect will be charged and usually released on bail. If there is not enough evidence to charge the suspect at that stage, they will be detained so that the police have time to gather the necessary evidence.

Time limits

The police are not allowed to detain a suspect indefinitely, and the custody officer is required to review the need for detention regularly. The custody officer will review whether there is enough evidence to charge after the first 6 hours. Further reviews are carried out every 9 hours. Generally, the police can detain suspects for up to 36 hours, timed from their arrival at the station. This may be extended for a further 12 hours by the police, but it must be an officer of superintendent rank or above. A further and final extension up to 96 hours is permitted, but this must be approved by a magistrate.

Search at the station

A suspect may be searched, or have samples taken, while at the police station. An example would be a breath or blood sample if drink driving were suspected. Again, the procedures are laid out in the relevant statutes, including PACE, and the person would have no claim for trespass against the person if such procedures were followed correctly.

Harassment

This area is governed by the **Protection from Harassment Act 1997**, as amended by the **Serious Organised Crime and Police Act 2005**.

Section 1 of the **Protection from Harassment Act 1997**, as amended, states that:

> A person must not pursue a course of conduct...which amounts to harassment of another, and...which he knows or ought to know amounts to harassment of the other.

Section 2 of the **Protection from Harassment Act 1997** states that the person whose course of conduct is in question ought to know that it amounts to or involves harassment of another, if a reasonable person in possession of the same information would think that it amounted to harassment. Thus, a defendant would not be able to argue that he/she did not intend to cause the victim harassment if a reasonable person, on the same facts, would realise that it would be the probable result.

A person who harasses another is guilty of a criminal offence, but the legislation also provides a civil remedy. The claimant may be awarded damages for any anxiety or financial loss caused by the harassment. Additionally, victims may apply for an injunction to restrain the person harassing them.

A Consent: *volenti non fit injuria*

On some occasions, consent of the victim may operate to prevent the defendant from incurring liability for what would otherwise be an offence. The definition of the Latin phrase '*volenti non fit injuria*' is 'to a willing person, no injury is done'. Often shortened to '*volenti*', this means that if a claimant has voluntarily undertaken the risk of harm, he/she can have no claim against the party who inflicted it. Examples include a hospital patient who agrees to an injection or a boxer who agrees to a boxing match. The patient would have no cause of action against the doctor who administered the injection, just as the boxer would have no claim against his/her opponent. In both cases, he/she voluntarily agrees to run the risk of the harm inflicted.

1 *Effect*

Volenti operates as a complete defence and the defendant will not incur any liability.

2 *Elements*

2.1 Consent must be given freely

For consent to operate as a defence, it must be given freely by the claimant. In *Bowater* v *Rowley Regis Corporation* (1944) (see below for facts), Scott LJ stated:

> For the purpose of the rule, if it be a rule, a man cannot be said to be truly 'willing' unless he is in a position to choose freely, and freedom of choice predicates, not only full knowledge of the circumstances on which the exercise of choice is conditioned, so that he may be able to choose wisely, but the absence from his mind of any feeling of constraint so that nothing shall interfere with the freedom of his will. Without purporting to lay down any rule of universal application, I venture to doubt whether the maxim can very often apply in circumstances of an injury to a servant by the negligence of his master.

Consent obtained by duress will be invalid.

2.2 Knowledge and understanding of the risks involved

In addition to the consent being given freely, the person consenting must know about and understand the risks involved if consent is to operate as a defence. The test is subjective — did the claimant have knowledge and understanding of the risk? He/she must know that the risk exists but also be aware of its nature and extent.

2.3 Types of consent

Consent can be either express or implied.

Consent: volenti non fit injuria

2.3a Express consent

A person may give his/her express consent in a number of ways, for example, by agreeing verbally or in writing to take the risk.

2.3b Implied consent

Sometimes, consent may be implied or inferred through circumstances or conduct. An example would be a boxer who turned up for a fight; an opponent would infer from the very fact that he/she had turned up that he/she consented to the fight.

The mere fact that a claimant is aware of a risk, however, is not conclusive proof that he/she consented to it.

Smith v *Baker* (1891)

The claimant was employed by the defendants to work at a quarry. A crane would often swing heavy stones over his head while he worked. He complained to his employers about this, so was obviously aware of the risk, but this did not prevent him from succeeding in a claim for negligence when he was injured by a stone that fell from the crane. His employers could not rely on *volenti* as a defence to their negligence. The claimant had not consented to the harm merely by knowing about the risk and, in reality, the House of Lords accepted that the claimant had little choice but to continue working in those conditions.

3 *Employers/employees*

The courts have also been asked in several other cases to decide whether employers can rely on the defence of *volenti* when their employees have been injured at work.

Bowater v *Rowley Regis Corporation* (1944)

The claimant was employed by the defendant corporation to collect rubbish in a horse and cart. Despite his protests, he was told to take out a dangerous horse. He sued his employers when he was injured after the horse bolted and he was thrown from the cart. The Court of Appeal did not allow the defendants to rely on *volenti*. It was not enough that the claimant had taken the horse — for *volenti* to operate, the claimant, knowing the danger, would have to *willingly* accept the risks involved.

There are occasions, however, when the courts *have* allowed defendant employers to rely on *volenti*.

The courts will not usually allow the defence of *volenti* in an employer–employee relationship.

ICI v *Shatwell* (1965)

Two brothers were employed as shot firers in the defendant's quarry. In breach of their employer's instructions — and indeed statutes and safety regulations — they did not follow the correct procedures when testing explosives and were both injured as a result when there was an explosion. The House of Lords held that the defence of *volenti* did apply here and as such, the employer was not negligent. The employees had undertaken the unsafe method of working entirely of their own accord and in breach of explicit instructions issued by their employer.

4 Consent to run the risk of injury

For the defendant to be able to rely on *volenti*, the claimant must have consented to run the legal risk of injury.

Nettleship v *Weston* (1971)

The claimant was a driving instructor who was injured when his pupil, the defendant, drove into a lamppost. It was held that *volenti* did not apply. Prior to the lessons, the claimant had asked the learner whether the car was insured in case there was an accident. The claimant had assured him that she had insurance that covered him as a passenger in the event of an accident. *Volenti* did not apply in this case as, in asking about the insurance, the instructor clearly showed that he did not agree to absolve the defendant from liability.

5 Road Traffic Act 1988

Section 149 of the **Road Traffic Act 1988** states that when it is compulsory to hold insurance, 'any antecedent agreement or understanding' between a driver and passenger shall have no effect. This means that if there is a road accident and the passenger is injured, the defendant cannot plead *volenti* — in other words, he or she cannot claim that by getting into the car the passenger agreed to the risk of injury. This does not appear to apply to all forms of transport.

Morris v *Murray* (1991)

The claimant and defendant spent the afternoon drinking. The claimant then agreed to accompany the defendant pilot on a flight in his light aircraft. The plane crashed, the pilot was killed and his passenger was injured. The claim for damages against the pilot's estate failed after the court held that *volenti* applied.

6 Rescuers

The courts give special consideration to rescuers, and it is rare that the defence of *volenti* will apply. This is because it is foreseeable that if a person is in need of assistance, someone would come to his/her aid and, as a result, may suffer physical or psychiatric harm. Additionally, a rescuer is not in a position to weigh up the situation and agree to the risk of such injury; indeed, he/she may have to act quickly with no time for consideration of personal danger. Also, it may not be a free choice for many — they may react instinctively or feel that they have no option but to act. Another matter for consideration is that the negligence occurred before the rescuer took the risk. Finally, it is difficult to see how a person could have consented to something that he/she may be unaware of — at the time of acting, a rescuer may not know that it was the defendant's negligence that caused the accident.

Haynes v *Harwood* (1935)

The defendants owned a two-horse van, which their employee left unattended in a street. A young boy threw a stone at the horses, causing them to run off down the street. The claimant policeman saw that a woman and several children were in danger and he was injured when he tried to stop the horses.

The Court of Appeal did not allow the defendants to rely on *volenti* — the claimant was under a general duty to act to protect the women and children.

Even the fact that the claimant is a professional rescuer, such as a member of an ambulance or fire crew, will not mean that he or she voluntarily accepted the risk of harm.

Salmon v *Seafarers' Restaurants* (1983)

The claimant fireman was successful in obtaining damages after he was injured when trying to put out a chip-shop fire caused by the defendant's negligence. *Volenti* did not apply, despite the fact that he was a professional rescuer employed to take such risks.

However, the courts will consider whether the actions of the rescuer were necessary in the circumstances.

Cutler v *United Dairies* (1933)

The claimant was injured trying to recapture horses that had escaped. The horses ran into a field where they posed no risk. The court allowed the defendant to rely on *volenti* — there was no emergency. The claimant was taken to have willingly accepted the risk of harm and was thus denied compensation.

7 ## *Sports*

As with trespass to the person, the general rule is that by agreeing to participate, competitors consent to the usual risks of a sport. Thus, if a claimant is playing rugby, cricket or football, for example, he/she cannot usually complain about any injury sustained, as long as it was within the rules of that particular game. If the injury was inflicted outside of the rules, however, consent will probably not be available as a defence.

Condon v *Basi* (1985)

The claimant and defendant were on opposing teams in an amateur football match. The claimant was awarded damages after sustaining serious injuries following a foul tackle by the defendant. Consent did not apply, as the defendant had acted outside of the rules of the game. He acted beyond what might reasonably be expected from a participant by showing a reckless disregard for the claimant's safety.

Volenti may also be applicable when a claimant is injured as a spectator at a sporting event.

Wooldridge v *Sumner* (1963)

The claimant was a spectator at a horse show who was injured after the defendant rode his horse too fast and lost control. Diplock LJ stated that:

> A person attending a game or competition takes the risk of any damage caused to him by any act of a participant done in the course of and for the purposes of the game or competition notwithstanding that such act may involve an error of judgement or lapse of skill, unless the participant's conduct is such as to evince a reckless disregard of the spectator's safety.

Sidebar notes:

Any other decisions would mean that a potential rescuer, prior to acting, would have to consider the fact that he/she may be injured and unable to claim compensation. Policy clearly comes into this area, as the courts do not want to discourage people from helping those in need.

The rules of the particular sport will be taken into account when deciding the limits of consent, but a breach will not always give rise to a claim in negligence.

Spectators attending sporting events are held to have voluntarily taken the risk of injury from the participants, as long as such injuries are not inflicted intentionally or recklessly.

B Contributory negligence

1 Nature

Everyone is expected to take reasonable care of his/her own safety or interests. Contributory negligence is relevant when the claimant has contributed in some way to the harm that he/she has suffered and is therefore partly to blame. A common example is that of a car passenger who fails to wear a seatbelt. If there is an accident as a result of the driver's negligence in which the claimant is injured, the courts will assess to what extent the claimant's failure to wear a seatbelt contributed to his/her injuries — would the injuries have been less serious or even avoided altogether if the claimant had been wearing a seatbelt? Many examples concern personal injury, but contributory negligence can also apply in economic loss cases.

It must first be established that the defendant was negligent before the level of fault on the part of the claimant can be assessed. Put simply, the defendant will be found to be negligent but will then argue that the claimant is partly responsible for the harm that he/she has suffered.

For a finding of contributory negligence, it must always be proved that the claimant's actions contributed to the harm that he/she suffered.

Woods v *Davidson* (1930)
There was no contributory negligence when a drunken claimant was run over by the defendant, as the evidence showed that the defendant would have hit him in any event, even if he had not been intoxicated.

Jones v *Livox Quarries Ltd* (1952)
The claimant was injured at work while standing on a tow bar on the back of a traxcavator vehicle when a colleague in another vehicle negligently drove into the back of it. The claimant said that he had only taken the obvious risk of falling off the back of the vehicle. If he had fallen off and been injured, then he would have been partly to blame. Since his injuries occurred in a different way — being hit from behind — he argued that there was no contributory negligence. The court disagreed and held that by standing on the tow bar he had risked not only falling off it but also the chance that he may be hit from behind by another vehicle. It would have been different if, for example, he had been riding on the tow bar and had been hit on the head by a rock — the fact that he was negligently riding on the tow bar would have no bearing on his injuries. A finding of contributory negligence was made and the claimant's damages were reduced.

2 Effect

If contributory negligence is found, the effect is a reduction in the amount of damages that the claimant receives. The full amount of damages that would have been awarded is calculated first. Next, a decision is made upon how much, in terms of a percentage, the claimant was to blame for the damage. Finally, that percentage amount is deducted from the full award. An example would be a claimant who would have been awarded £10,000 in damages but who was found to have been 50% contributory negligent. He/she would then receive £5,000 damages rather than the full amount. As the defendant must be shown to be liable before an assessment of contributory negligence is made, damages can never be reduced by 100% so that the claimant receives nothing — both the defendant and the claimant must be to blame.

3 Law Reform (Contributory Negligence) Act 1945

The relevant statute in this area is the **Law Reform (Contributory Negligence) Act 1945**. Before this statute was passed, under common law, if the claimant was partly responsible for the damage sustained, he/she did not receive any compensation whatsoever. This statute was introduced to end the 'all or nothing' approach that had led to unfairness. Section 1(1) states:

> Where any person suffers damage as the result partly of his own fault and partly of the fault of any other person or persons...the damages recoverable...shall be reduced to such extent as the court thinks just and equitable having regard to the claimant's share in the responsibility for the damage.

The reduction depends on the facts in each case, but the courts have laid down guidelines for cases of road accidents in which the claimant has not been wearing a seatbelt.

Froom v *Butcher* (1976)
The claimant was involved in a collision when the defendant's car, which was speeding on the wrong side of the road, crashed into his vehicle. The claimant was not wearing a seatbelt and suffered more serious injuries than he would have done had he been wearing the restraint. The Court of Appeal laid down set percentages by which damages would be reduced in such cases.

If wearing a seatbelt would:
- not have made any difference to the injuries sustained — no reduction
- have lessened the severity of the injuries — 15% reduction
- have prevented the injuries — 25% reduction

O'Connell v *Jackson* (1972)
The same applies to motorcyclists whose injuries are more severe because they did not wear a crash helmet.

4 Standard of care

The claimant is expected to meet the standard of the reasonable person engaged in that activity — he/she must take proper care for his/her own safety in all the circumstances. It is when he/she falls below this standard that the matter of contributory negligence arises. As in ordinary negligence, this is an objective standard, but the courts will make allowances — for example, a frail elderly person would not be expected to cross the road as quickly as a younger, fitter person. Allowances are made most notably for children.

Gough v *Thorne* (1966)

A 13-year-old girl was killed while crossing the road. The driver of a lorry had signalled for her to cross, which she did without any further checks. A negligent motorist hit her, but the court found that in this case there was no contributory negligence — the girl had reached the standard of care of a child of the same age.

In this case, Lord Denning stated:

> A very young child cannot be guilty of contributory negligence. An older child may be; but it depends on the circumstances. A judge should only find a child guilty of contributory negligence if he or she is of such an age as reasonably to be expected to take precautions for his or her own safety: and then he or she is only to be found guilty if blame should be attached to him or her. A child has not the road sense or the experience of his or her elders.

Yachuk v *Oliver Blais and Co.* (1949)

A 9-year-old boy bought petrol from the defendants and was badly burned while playing with it. While the defendants were negligent in selling the petrol to him, there was no contributory negligence on his part since he was too young to appreciate the dangers involved.

Evans v *Souls Garage* (2000)

A 13-year-old who was burned playing with petrol sold to him by the defendants had his damages reduced by a third because of contributory negligence, as he could appreciate the dangers involved in such activity.

The courts will also take into account the circumstances, and will not usually punish a claimant who merely made a mistake — especially if it was in the heat of the moment.

Jones v *Boyce* (1816)

The claimant was a passenger on the defendant's coach. One of the reins broke and the claimant jumped off when it seemed as though the coach was about to topple over. The claimant broke his leg as a result. In fact, the coach did not overturn. The defendant argued that had the claimant remained where he was, he would not have broken his leg, and therefore the claimant was to blame for his own injuries. The court did not find contributory negligence in this case — the claimant had acted as a reasonable and prudent man would have done.

If the actions of the defendant increase the chance of the claimant making a mistake, the degree of contributory negligence will be assessed accordingly.

Brannon v *Airtours* (1999)

The defendant holiday company organised an entertainment evening with unlimited free wine where excessive drinking was encouraged. The claimant was injured when, despite warnings, he climbed onto a table and was hit by a ceiling fan. At the original trial, contributory negligence on the part of the claimant was assessed at 75%, since he had ignored warnings not to stand on the tables. On appeal, the Court of Appeal agreed that the defendant company was negligent in encouraging its clients to drink too much, and the claimant was held to be only 50% to blame for his injuries. This was because the defendant had encouraged an atmosphere of excessive drinking, despite being aware that this would make its clients less careful.

Children are expected to reach the standard of an ordinary child of the same age. This is a lower standard than that expected for adults.

Remember that before contributory negligence can apply, it must be shown that the defendant was negligent.

5 Drunk drivers

If a passenger accepts a lift from a driver whom he/she knows to be drunk, he/she may be found to have contributed to any injuries he/she suffers in the event of an accident. The defendant must prove that the claimant was aware that he/she was not fit to drive.

Owens v *Brimmel* (1977)

The claimant and defendant had both been on a pub crawl before the defendant attempted to drive home. During the journey, the car left the road and the claimant was seriously injured. The court found that the claimant was 20% to blame for his injuries. As they had both been drinking together, the claimant knew that the defendant was drunk when he accepted the lift and he was aware of the potential dangers.

6 Multiple defendants

If the claimant and two or more defendants are all responsible for the claimant's injuries, the courts will apportion liability according to their degree of blameworthiness.

Fitzgerald v *Lane* (1989)

The claimant was injured when he crossed the road when it was not safe to do so and was hit by two different negligent drivers. All three parties — the claimant and both drivers — were to blame. The House of Lords held that the correct way to assess damages was to calculate the full award and then assess contributory negligence on the claimant's part. The full award should then be reduced by the amount that the claimant was to blame for his/her own injuries. Finally, the remaining sum should be divided between the defendants, according to how blameworthy they each were.

As an example, damages in a case may be calculated at £1,000. Contributory negligence may be assessed at 20%. This means that as the claimant is 20% to blame he is entitled to only 80% of the full award — £800. This sum must be paid by the defendants. If the courts decide that defendant 1 is 10% to blame and defendant 2 is 90% to blame, defendant 1 will pay £80 and defendant 2 will pay the remaining £720.

Summary of Topic 9

Consent: *volenti non fit injuria*

On some occasions, consent of the victim may operate to prevent the defendant from incurring liability for what would otherwise be an offence. The definition of the Latin phrase '*volenti non fit injuria*' is 'to a willing person, no injury is done'. Often shortened to '*volenti*', this means that if a claimant has voluntarily undertaken the risk of harm, he/she can have no claim against the party who inflicted it.

Effect

Volenti operates as a complete defence and the defendant will not incur any liability.

Elements

Consent must be given freely

For consent to operate as a defence, it must be given freely by the claimant. Consent obtained by duress will be invalid.

Knowledge and understanding of the risks involved

In addition to the consent being given freely, the person consenting must know about and understand the risks involved if consent is to operate as a defence. The test is subjective — did the claimant have knowledge and understanding of the risk?

Types of consent

Consent can be either express or implied.

Express consent

A person may give his/her express consent in a number of ways, for example, by agreeing verbally or in writing to take the risk.

Implied consent

Sometimes, consent may be implied or inferred through circumstances or conduct. An example would be a boxer who turned up for a fight; an opponent would infer from the very fact that he/she had turned up that he/she consented to the fight. The mere fact that a claimant is aware of a risk, however, is not conclusive proof that he/she consented to it (*Smith* v *Baker*, 1891).

Employers/employees

The courts will not usually allow the defence of *volenti* in an employer–employee relationship, but it has been accepted on some occasions (*ICI* v *Shatwell*, 1965).

Consent to run the risk of injury

For the defendant to be able to rely on *volenti*, the claimant must have consented to run the legal risk of injury (*Nettleship* v *Weston*, 1971).

Road Traffic Act 1988

Section 149 of the **Road Traffic Act 1988** states that when it is compulsory to hold insurance, 'any antecedent agreement or understanding' between a driver and passenger shall have no effect. This does not appear to apply to all forms of transport (*Morris* v *Murray*, 1991).

Rescuers

The courts give special consideration to rescuers, and it is rare that the defence of *volenti* will apply.

Even the fact that the claimant is a professional rescuer, such as a member of an ambulance or fire crew, will not mean that he/she voluntarily accepted the risk of harm (*Salmon* v *Seafarers' Restaurants*, 1983).

Sports

The general rule is that by agreeing to participate, competitors consent to the usual risks of a sport. If the injury was inflicted outside of the rules, however, consent will probably not be available as a defence. *Volenti* may also be applicable when a claimant is injured at a sporting event (*Wooldridge* v *Sumner*, 1963).

Contributory negligence

Nature

Everyone is expected to take reasonable care of his/her own safety or interests. Contributory negligence is relevant when the claimant has contributed in some way to the harm that he/she has suffered and is therefore partly to blame. Many examples concern personal injury, but contributory negligence can also apply in economic loss cases.

It must first be established that the defendant was negligent before the level of fault on the part of the claimant can be assessed. Put simply, the defendant will be found to be negligent but will then argue that the claimant is partly responsible for the harm that he/she has suffered. For a finding of contributory negligence, it must always be proved that the claimant's actions contributed to the harm that he or she suffered (*Woods* v *Davidson*, 1930 and *Jones* v *Livox Quarries Ltd*, 1952).

Effect

If contributory negligence is found, the effect is a reduction in the amount of damages that the claimant receives. The full amount of damages that would have been awarded is calculated first. Next, a decision is made upon how much, in terms of a percentage, the claimant was to blame for the damage. Finally, that percentage amount is deducted from the full award.

Law Reform (Contributory Negligence) Act 1945

The relevant statute for contributory negligence is the **Law Reform (Contributory Negligence) Act 1945**. Before this statute was passed, under common law, if the claimant was partly responsible for the damage sustained, he/she did not receive any compensation. This statute was introduced to end the 'all or nothing' approach that had led to unfairness. The reduction depends on the facts in each case, but the courts have laid down guidelines in some instances, e.g. for road accidents when the claimant has not been wearing a seatbelt (*Froom* v *Butcher*, 1976).

Standard of care

The claimant is expected to meet the standard of the reasonable person engaged in that activity — he/she must take proper care for his/her own safety in all the circumstances. As in ordinary negligence, this is an objective standard, but the courts will make allowances — for example, a frail elderly person would not be expected to cross the road as quickly as a younger, fitter person. Allowances are made most notably for children, who are expected to reach the standard of an ordinary child of the same age (*Gough* v *Thorne*, 1966). The courts will also take into account the circumstances, and will not usually punish a claimant who merely made a mistake — especially if it was in the heat of the moment (*Jones* v *Boyce*, 1816).

Drunk drivers

If a passenger accepts a lift from a driver whom he/she knows to be drunk, he/she may be found to have contributed to any injuries he/she suffers in an accident. The defendant must prove that the claimant was aware that he/she was not fit to drive.

Multiple defendants

If the claimant and two or more defendants are all responsible for the claimant's injuries, the courts will apportion liability according to their degree of blameworthiness.

Civil law should not seek to find people guilty and punish them; instead, it should be concerned with finding remedies.

Remedies are ways of solving disputes between parties:
- If a motorist is negligent and crashes into another car, the owner of that car would want **damages** (money).
- If a person is constantly being disturbed by his/her neighbour's loud music, he/she may want an **injunction** (a court order).

A Damages

The aim of awarding damages is usually to compensate a person, i.e. to put him/her back in the position he/she was in before the tort was committed. For example, if a motorist has negligently caused £1,000 worth of damage to someone's car, compensatory damages for that amount would be awarded to the other person. Sometimes the courts will award lower damages (contemptuous damages) or higher damages (aggravated damages and exemplary damages).

1 Compensatory damages

This is the most common remedy sought in a civil case. When calculating the amount of compensation, the judge will consider two types of damages: general and special.

1.1 General damages

General damages are for injury and losses where it is difficult to give an exact price. They are also known as non-pecuniary losses. There are tariff guidelines issued by the Court of Appeal for the amount of compensation that a person suffering from different injuries can claim, but the amount of compensation will vary with different circumstances.

It is difficult for the courts to compensate pain and suffering. Such claims can only be made for the time that the claimant could appreciate the pain and suffering. For example, a person cannot claim pain and suffering for the time that he/she spent in a coma.

***Hicks* v *South Yorkshire Police* (1992)**
Compensation for pain and suffering was not awarded to the victims of the Hillsborough disaster who were killed. The court decided that their deaths were quick.

General damages will also compensate for loss of amenity, such as an inability to play sport after an injury, impaired senses or impaired sexual enjoyment. Loss of amenity differs from pain and suffering in that it can be claimed while the claimant is unaware of the loss (e.g. when he/she is in a coma).

Claimants suffering from whiplash after a car accident usually receive a standard amount of compensation.

West and Son v *Shephard* (1964)

A claimant who was left unconscious and paralysed was awarded £17,500 for loss of amenity. She was unable to communicate, but there was medical evidence to suggest that she had some appreciation of her circumstances.

Loss of future earnings is particularly difficult to calculate. The courts have to guess for how long the claimant would have worked if he/she had not been injured and whether he/she would have been promoted or made unemployed. The damages are awarded as a lump sum, which when invested as an annuity will give the claimant an income for life or for the duration that the injury is likely to last.

The claimant's net annual loss is the difference between his/her income before the injury and the income (if any) that he/she receives afterwards. Some claimants will not be able to work at all, whereas others may be able to work in a lower-paid job. The multiplicand is the amount that the court thinks the claimant's earning would have altered, e.g. through promotion or changing job. The multiplier is the amount of money required to invest that will give the annual income that the claimant is entitled to. These two amounts calculate the loss of earnings.

Multiplicand × multiplier = loss of earnings compensation

Doyle v *Wallace* (1998)

The claimant was unable to work after a car accident. She was intending to train to be a teacher, but if she did not pass the exams she planned to do clerical work. The court estimated that she had a 50% chance of becoming a teacher. They awarded her loss of earnings that was halfway between what she would have earned in clerical work and what she would have earned as a teacher.

Damages for fatal accidents are calculated using the **Fatal Accidents Act 1976**. Dependants can claim for financial losses that they have incurred from the claimant's death. The defendant may have to compensate the deceased's dependants.

Martin and Brown v *Grey* (1998)

The 12-year-old daughter of a woman who was killed was awarded compensation to provide the services of a mother.

1.2 Special damages

Pecuniary means money.

The courts are able to calculate special damages exactly (they are also known as pecuniary losses). Special damages include loss of earnings up to the date of the trial, medical expenses, damage to property and any other loss that the claimant might have incurred.

When property is destroyed, the claimant will receive its market value.

2 Contemptuous damages

The court may show disapproval of a claimant's decision to take a case to court in the first place. If the judge believes that the case should never have made it to court, he/she may award the winner contemptuous damages.

Pamplin v *Express Newspapers Ltd* (1988)

The claimant sued the *Daily Express* for defamation when it called him 'sleazy'. Pamplin had avoided paying parking tickets by registering his car in the name of his infant son. Although the court found in favour of Pamplin, the judge only awarded him the lowest coin of the realm, which in 1988 was half a pence.

3 Aggravated damages

The amount of damages awarded may be increased if the defendant aggravated the claimant's injuries. According to Lord Devlin in *Rookes* v *Barnard* (1964), this includes humiliating the claimant or acting out of spite.

Ansell v *Thomas* (1974)
The claimant received aggravated damages because the police humiliated him when they wrongfully dragged him out of his business in front of his employees.

4 Exemplary damages

Such an award is criticised, as the civil law should not seek to punish.

Exemplary damages are also supposed to make an example of the unsuccessful party and serve as a deterrent to others who may be considering doing the same.

Exemplary damages are punitive. They seek to punish the unsuccessful party in a civil case by awarding the winner more damages than are necessary to compensate him/her.

Cassell v *Broome* (1972)
The defendant made a libellous comment in his book about the claimant being a coward in the Second World War. The defendant calculated that he would still make a profit out of the book even after he had compensated the claimant. The courts saw this as behaviour that should not be encouraged. They therefore made the defendant pay exemplary damages so that he did not profit from his tort.

Rookes v *Barnard* (1964)
The House of Lords stated that exemplary damages may be awarded when:
- a statute allows such an award
- the defendant calculated that he/she would still make a profit after compensating the claimant (as in *Cassell* v *Broome*)
- a government official acted oppressively (as in *Russell McName and McCotter* v *Home Office*, 2001, where prison officers beat up an IRA prisoner who had escaped from prison)

The Law Commission Report 1997 recommended that the rule on exemplary damages should apply to all types of tort. In the recent case of *Kuddus* v *Chief Constable Leicestershire Constabulary* (2001), the House of Lords had the same view.

B Injunctions

The claimant in a civil case may want a court order that either forces the defendant to stop a certain activity or to make him/her do something. In the tort of nuisance, injunctions are a common remedy. If a neighbour is causing a nuisance by playing music too loud, an injunction may stop him/her from playing it at certain times of day. However, if a neighbour's trees are blocking the sunlight to other houses, an injunction could force them to prune the tree.

Equity is when cases are decided according to what is fair for both parties rather than the judge following strict legal rules.

The court will not grant an injunction if damages would be more appropriate. The court may also award damages as well as an injunction. An injunction will only be granted when it is equitable (fair) to do so, and courts will not make injunctions for trivial matters.

Llandudno UDC v *Woods* (1899)

The court refused to grant an injunction to stop people preaching on the beach, as it was regarded as a trivial matter.

There are different names for the types of injunction:
- A **mandatory** injunction forces the defendant to do something, e.g. prune a tree.
- A **prohibitory** injunction prevents the defendant from committing a tort, e.g. from playing his/her music.
- An **interim** injunction is granted before the trial in the time leading up to when the judge will consider the case fully.

Injunctions can also be full or partial.
- A full injunction prevents the defendant from committing the tort again.
- A partial injunction allows the defendant to commit the tort in certain circumstances.

Kennaway v *Thompson* (1980)

The claimant complained that a motorboat club was causing a nuisance to her lakeside property. The court decided that the noise from the boat club meetings and competitions *was* a nuisance and limited the club's activities instead of stopping them altogether.

Summary of Topic 10

Damages

The aim of awarding damages is usually to compensate a person, i.e. to put him/her back in the position he/she was in before the tort was committed.

Compensatory damages

This is the most common remedy sought in a civil case. When calculating the amount of compensation, the judge will consider two types of damages: general and special.

General damages

General damages are for injury and losses where it is difficult to give an exact price, for example:
- pain and suffering (*Hicks* v *South Yorkshire Police*, 1992)
- loss of amenity (*West and Son* v *Shephard*, 1964)
- loss of future earnings (multiplicand × multiplier = loss of earnings compensation)
- fatal accidents when the dependants require compensation (*Martin and Brown* v *Grey*, 1998)

Special damages

Special damages include loss of earnings up to the date of the trial, medical expenses, damage to property and any other loss that the claimant may have incurred.

Aggravated damages

The amount of damages awarded may be increased if the defendant aggravated the claimant's injuries. According to Lord Devlin in *Rookes* v *Barnard* (1964), this includes humiliating the claimant or acting out of spite (*Ansell* v *Thomas*, 1974).

Exemplary damages

Exemplary damages seek to punish the unsuccessful party in a civil case by awarding the winner more damages than are necessary to compensate him/her (*Cassell* v *Broome*, 1972 and *Rookes* v *Barnard*, 1964).

Contemptuous damages

Contemptuous damages show the court's disapproval of a claimant's decision to take a case to court in the first place (*Pamplin* v *Express Newspapers Ltd*, 1988).

Injunctions

The court will not grant an injunction if damages would be more appropriate. The court may also award damages as well as an injunction. An injunction will only be granted when it is equitable (fair) to do so and courts will not make injunctions for trivial matters (*Llandudno UDC* v *Woods*, 1899).

There are different names for the types of injunction:
- A **mandatory** injunction forces the defendant to do something, e.g. prune a tree.
- A **prohibitory** injunction prevents the defendant from committing a tort, e.g. from playing his/her music.
- An **interim** injunction is granted before the trial in the time leading up to when the judge will consider the case fully.

Injunctions can also be full or partial.
- A full injunction prevents the defendant from committing the tort again.
- A partial injunction allows the defendant to commit the tort in certain circumstances (*Kennaway* v *Thompson*, 1980).